TECHNIQUES
OF
BRIEF
PSYCHOTHERAPY

D0814065

TECHNIQUES OF BRIEF PSYCHOTHERAPY

Walter V. Flegenheimer, M.D.

JASON ARONSON INC.
Northvale, New Jersey
London

CREDITS

pp. 21–22   From *Studies on Hysteria* by Josef Breuer and Sigmund Freud. Translated from the German and edited by James Strachey, in collaboration with Anna Freud, assisted by Alix Strachey and Alan Tyson. Published in the United States by Basic Books, Inc., by arrangement with The Hogarth Press. By permission of Basic Books, Inc.

pp. 67, 70–71, 72–73   Reprinted by permission from *Short-Term Psychotherapy and Emotional Crisis* by Peter Sifneos. Published by Harvard University Press. Copyright © 1972 by the President and Fellows of Harvard College.

pp. 88–89, 90–92, 96–97   Reprinted by permission from *Time-Limited Psychotherapy* by James Mann. Published by Harvard University Press. Copyright © 1973 by the President and Fellows of Harvard College.

pp. 128–129, 134–138   Reprinted by permission from pages 296–297 and pages 348–351 in *Basic Principles and Techniques in Short-Term Dynamics Psychotherapy* by Habib Davanloo (ed.). Copyright © 1978, Spectrum Publications, Inc., New York City.

The Master Work Series

Copyright © 1993, 1982 by Walter V. Flegenheimer

First softcover edition 1993

All rights reserved. Printed in the United States of America. No part of this book may be used or reproduced in any manner whatsoever without written permission from Jason Aronson Inc. except in the case of brief quotations in reviews for inclusion in a magazine, newspaper, or broadcast.

Library of Congress Cataloging-in-Publication Data

Flegenheimer, Walter V.
   Techniques of brief psychotherapy.
   Bibliography: p. 193
   Includes index.
   1. Psychotherapy, Brief.   I. Title [DNLM:
1. Psychotherapy, Brief—Methods.   WM 420 F595t]
RC480.55.F58   1983   616.89′14   82-13891

ISBN 0-87668-496-7 (hardcover)
ISBN 1-56821-095-7 (softcover)

Manufactured in the United States of America. Jason Aronson Inc. offers books and cassettes. For information and catalog write to Jason Aronson Inc., 230 Livingston Street, Northvale, New Jersey 07647.

For those whose skillful work with patients
led to the current interest in brief psychotherapy.

Habib Davanloo
David Malan
James Mann
Peter Sifneos
Lewis Wolberg

"being under sentence of termination doth most marvelously concentrate the material"

David Malan
after Samuel Johnson

CONTENTS

PREFACE

Brief psychotherapy is as old as psychotherapy itself. Even in the modern era of psychotherapy, that is, the period since Freud's initial discoveries in the 1890s, brief psychotherapy has been a part of the clinician's armamentarium; yet during this time brief psychotherapy was often in disrepute— a second-class mode of treatment which would do only if nothing better was available. As psychotherapy developed during the 20th century, various schools and orientations of therapy became established, and each generated its own form of brief psychotherapy. As a result, the published literature, including papers on brief forms of individual, group, and family therapies covering a wide range of orientations, now consists of over one thousand diverse entries. All of these therapies cannot be considered in a single volume in any meaningful way. This book is limited to a discussion of psychoanalytically oriented individual brief psychotherapies.

The current interest in psychoanalytically oriented brief psychotherapy grew out of work that began in the late 1950s and early 1960s. In that period most training centers were treating a small number of patients with long-term psychoanalytically oriented psychotherapy. Because many people wanted treatment, long waiting lists of unserved patients were common, and techniques of brief treatment were developed as an expedient alternative to long-term therapy. It was soon noted, however, that in addition to helping reduce waiting lists and meet the requirements of third-party payers, these new techniques were also often remarkably effective and could, in some cases, produce results comparable to those of long-term therapy. Some of these techniques have been refined and used in the subsequent years, and their early promise has been substantiated by the good results that are still being achieved.

It has become clear that not only mild symptoms of recent onset can be treated with brief psychotherapy, but also that many people with long-standing, relatively severe symptoms or complaints can be helped with these techniques. Brief psychotherapy is efficacious, and for some patients it is the treatment of choice. Indeed, brief therapy may be the only effective form of treatment that a patient will accept. Psychoanalysis and long-term psychotherapy are being used more and more to treat patients whose psychopathology requires dealing with complicated pregenital issues that involve the early stages of libidinal development and the vicissitudes of the formation of self- and object representations. While many patients show this type of psychopathology, there is a need for a therapy designed to deal with conflicts which affect people whose early development was relatively benign. Brief psychotherapy can often meet that need.

Brief psychotherapy is now an important part of many training programs, and there is widespread interest in this topic in the profession. The rich material that the patient produces in the time available and the intense affect that is mobilized during the treatment can make brief psychotherapy a more exciting and rewarding experience for the therapist than long-term psychotherapy. Brief psychotherapy, because its parameters are relatively easy to control, is a useful research tool for studying the mechanisms of *any* psychotherapy.

The major brief therapy techniques which are in use today are the subject of this book. Because these therapies were developed independently of one another, they each differ in terms of selection criteria and specific techniques of treatment; so learning about one technique does not provide the student with information about the other techniques. Heretofore, the material on these therapies has not been available in a single volume. Each therapist published his or her own work, usually in book form; very little of the work was published in professional journals. Therefore, anyone who wished to become familiar with this subject had to study many separate volumes. This book describes all the major current systems of brief psychotherapy in sufficient detail for the reader to obtain a clear picture of each technique. While this book will not turn the reader into an accomplished brief psychotherapist, it will provide enough information so that one can decide which, if any, of the systems one may wish to pursue further in order to become proficient in its practice.

The major systems of brief psychotherapy being used and taught at this time are those of Davanloo, Malan, Mann, and Sifneos. The work of Alexander is included, not only because of its great historical importance, but also because the flexibility of approach which Alexander advocated and demonstrated may appeal to those readers who do not feel comfortable with some of the more systematized approaches of the other authors. Wolberg is included because his contributions to the process of working through are relevant to all forms of brief psychotherapy.

The book is organized so that the first chapter, "The Essential Elements of Brief Psychotherapy," serves as an introduction to the following ones, and it is recommended that it be read before any of the others, unless the reader is already quite familiar with the subject. All the other chapters can be read independently of one another, except for Chapter 9, which presupposes a knowledge of the preceding chapters. A summary is provided for the chapters on technique so that the reader can quickly see which chapters are of interest to him or her.

My own knowledge of the field is derived from several sources. Since 1974 I have taught crisis intervention and brief psychotherapy to second-year residents at the Mount Sinai School of Medicine in New York City, presenting didactic material, leading group discussions, and supervising individual resident's brief psychotherapy experiences. I have treated patients with brief psychotherapy in my private psychiatric practice. I have attended workshops and courses given by Davanloo, Malan, Mann, and Sifneos in order to supplement my readings with personal observations of the style of each therapist. While in my own clinical work I generally prefer to use either Mann's or Malan's method, I have tried in this volume to present each technique as impartially as possible, hoping to reflect the point of view of the therapist under discussion.

ACKNOWLEDGMENTS

I would like to thank Jason Aronson, without whose persistence this book would not have been written. I also want to thank Hannah Flegenheimer and Joan Langs for their excellent editorial assistance, and Susan Morance, who not only typed the manuscript but also made many helpful corrections along the way.

1

THE ESSENTIAL ELEMENTS OF BRIEF PSYCHOTHERAPY

Successful analytically oriented brief psychotherapy requires both a properly selected patient and a therapist trained in the appropriate technique. Some of the requirements for patient and therapist are identical with those needed for analytically oriented long-term therapy, while other requirements are unique to the short-term mode of treatment. Although the authors discussed in the following chapters have their own modifications of selection procedures and technique, there are certain elements that are common to all of these brief approaches. These common elements have recently been summarized by Marmor (1979), and the following discussion in general follows his outline. While the various factors will be presented separately, it is important to note that brief psychotherapy is effective because of the interaction of all these factors.

SELECTION OF PATIENTS

GENERAL FACTORS

It is ironic that the best patients for brief psychotherapy are those who would also be considered the best patients for long-term psychotherapy by therapists unfamiliar with brief psychotherapy. As will be discussed, this situation has hindered the growth and wider application of brief psychotherapy. A relatively healthy, well-functioning patient with a well-defined and circumscribed area of difficulty, who is intelligent, psychologically minded, and well motivated for change is someone who would gladden the heart of any therapist, and such a person is the best candidate for brief psychotherapy.

How healthy should someone be to be considered for brief psychotherapy? While the various authors differ on the details, in general, psychotic, severely depressed, and borderline patients, as well as those with severe character disorders, are excluded. This does not mean, however, that only patients with mild symptoms or with symptomatology of recent onset can be treated by these methods. Malan (1976a) reviewed the controversy between the conservative brief psychotherapists who feel only recent symptoms of mild or moderate severity can be treated with brief techniques, and the radical brief psychotherapists who believe that in properly selected patients extensive and long-standing psychopathology can be treated with brief techniques. Malan concluded that the evidence is clear that the radical position is the correct one. He emphasized that this does not mean that the milder cases may not also be helped, but it does mean that brief psychotherapy does not have to be *limited* to the milder cases. If the selection criteria are matched to the appropriate techniques, a wide range of diagnoses can be handled with these treatment modalities, leading to results which include not only symptom removal or amelioration, but also some characterological changes, as well as changes in the patient's characteristic modes of defense. As can be seen, the goals of brief psychotherapy *can* be similar to the goals of long-term psychotherapy, although, of course, this is not always the case.

The better the individual's functioning in his or her past and current life situation, the more likely is such a person to benefit from psychotherapy, provided other selection factors are also present. Thus, a person who has shown enough perseverance and stability to succeed in his or her schooling and vocation, who has shown the ability to establish and maintain a close interpersonal relationship, and who demonstrates sufficient intelligence to deal with the type of concepts required in insight-oriented psychotherapy is a person evidencing sufficient ego-strength to be considered for this type of treatment. While the patient's current functioning is a measure of ego-strength, it is also a measure of the stability of his or her real life situation, and this is an important factor in considering people for brief psychotherapy. While this factor is implied in many selection criteria, it has not been sufficiently stressed that a person's current life should be in relative order for brief treatment to be beneficial. Both patient and therapist generally deal first with the real events of the patient's current life, and if it is filled with constant turmoil, for example unemployment, moving, broken relationships, difficulty with family, etcetera, there will often be little time left during the allotted hours to deal with the patient's underlying conflicts. Long-term therapy provides the leisure for dealing with things "later"; short-term therapy does not.

Psychological mindedness is another criterion for selecting a patient for any type of insight-oriented psychotherapy. It is always an advantage if the patient has some real insight into his or her problems, has some experience with introspection, and recognizes that past events are having some influence on present feelings and behavior. In long-term treatment, if these qualities are present in a minimal way, and there is sufficient motivation to assure that the patient remains in treatment, the therapist can feel fairly confident that, over a period of time, insight and psychological mindedness can be developed as the treatment unfolds and as the therapist is able to show the patient manifestations of his or her unconscious life. In short-term therapy, again, this luxury of time is not available, so that for most brief techniques a higher degree of psychological awareness is required from the outset. The usual manner of testing for this is through the use of trial interpretations during the evaluation period. It is important that the patient respond to the trial interpretation both intellectually and with the appropriate affect. If the response lacks the affectual component the treatment might easily become a meaningless intellectual exercise.

It is generally agreed that the patient–therapist interaction is crucial in any dynamic therapy. A therapeutic alliance requiring some positive feeling for the therapist and the treatment on the part of the patient must be established. Ideally, there is evidence for the formation of this alliance from the outset, but in long-term therapy, if the therapist has an understanding of the defenses involved, he or she can plan to work with these defenses until a good working alliance can be established. Again, in brief therapy there is generally not sufficient time to work through extensive defenses, so that evidence of a good relationship between patient and therapist should be present from the beginning. This does not mean that the presence of initial hostility or withdrawal automatically disqualifies the patient, but it does mean that, in addition to these resistances, the therapist should have some evidence of the patient's positive interaction with the therapist.

Similarly, as will be seen, the treatment, when it goes well, is an intensely affect-laden experience for both patient and therapist. It is therefore necessary that the patient have the ability to be in touch with his or her own feelings and to experience feelings in relation to another person. In long-term treatment, if it is felt that the capacity for relating and feeling is there but defended against, this can be worked with, while in brief treatment one looks for the capacity to relate and feel during the initial interview. It can be seen from the above discussion that much goes on during the initial evaluation for brief psychotherapy. It is apparent that the therapist must be much more active than the traditional long-term therapist in order to obtain the needed data. Indeed, the activity of the initial interview sets the tone for the activity of the therapist throughout the treatment. This will be discussed in more detail in the section on technique.

While all psychotherapy requires the patient to be motivated, a higher degree of motivation is necessary for brief psychotherapy in order to enable the patient to overcome his or her resistances and accomplish the tasks of the treatment in the time allotted. The greater the resistances and the more ambitious the therapeutic goals, the stronger must be the patient's motivation. In few brief therapy cases is there sufficient time to work through deep ambivalence concerning the wish to change; so it is important that the patient show clear evidence of this wish during the initial evaluation. The various workers have established different criteria to measure the patient's motivation, but they all agree that it is necessary that the patient show evidence of his or her wish to change maladaptive patterns and learn something about himself or herself so that new and better ways of coping may be chosen.

This is in contrast to the patient who just wishes for symptom removal without any work being required on his or her part. The latter patient will not do well with the type of brief psychotherapy described in this book.

THE FOCUS

What clearly sets brief psychotherapy apart from long-term psychotherapy is the requirement of working within a focus in the brief technique. A focus is a circumscribed symptom or area of difficulty, the resolution of which will satisfy the present needs of the patient. That is, if the problems of the focus can be resolved, the patient will feel that the therapy has been successful. For example, a man might be satisfied with a therapy that enables him to maintain satisfactory relationships with women, while it does nothing about his general tendency to procrastinate and leaves his mild travel phobia intact.

Generally, patient and therapist agree on what the focus will be at the start of the treatment and agree to concentrate their work on the area of the focus. It often happens that, as the therapy progresses, the focus will be modified, but in the properly selected patient, it will rarely have to be changed entirely. Thus, in the example given above, it may become apparent once therapy has begun that the patient has difficulty with men in authority and that this is related to his difficulty with women. His difficulty with authority will then be included within the focus. Of course, other symptoms or problem areas will emerge, but if they cannot be intimately connected with the focus, they are not pursued. If no focus can be determined—if the patient's complaints are vague, diffuse, or cover many aspects of life and functioning—brief psychotherapy is contraindicated.

So far the focus has been considered only in terms of current complaints on the part of the patient, but to be therapeutically meaningful the focus must be important dynamically as well. In the ideal patient the focus represents the current manifestations of the patient's nuclear conflict; that is, it is the chief remaining evidence of the patient's childhood neurosis. Again, in the ideal case, the therapist can trace a meaningful pattern from his or her understanding of the patient's childhood, through areas of similar difficulty in the past life of the patient, to the current focus.

There is much discussion in the brief psychotherapy literature about whether a focus is oedipal or preoedipal, though these concepts have not been clearly defined. Sifneos, for one, limits his patients to those who demonstrate a clearly oedipal focus. In general, conflicts involving three people, such as oedipal conflicts and sibling rivalry for primacy with a parent, lend themselves to resolution through brief therapy. Most workers will also treat patients whose chief childhood conflicts concern problems of loss, dependency versus independence, or other dyadic situations. The metapsychology of brief psychotherapy is at a very early stage of development, and the theoretical framework for the determination of a suitable dynamic focus does not really exist as yet. In practical terms, what happens is that when the other criteria for selection are adhered to, a patient selected for brief psychotherapy is one whose major conflicts developed at a rather advanced stage of psychosexual development; or if the conflicts developed earlier, they did not seriously interfere with the patient's subsequent development. Whether the conflict that now manifests itself in the symptoms of the focus is a triadic or dyadic one seems less important than the overall maturity or ego-strength that the patient has shown throughout his or her life.

It can be seen that the selection of the focus is critical to the outcome of the therapy. In some cases the focus is clear and there are no problems. But at times the true focus is hidden within a body of generalized complaints, and only skillful interviewing will make the focus evident. At other times, what appears to be a clear symptomatic focus is impossible to relate to the developmental history. If, after extensive history taking, the connection between the focus and the past has still not been elucidated, this is usually an indication that more serious psychopathology is present, and the patient is probably not suitable for brief psychotherapy. Sometimes, an interview with a therapist of a different sex will help clarify the situation. Patients with isolated delusions, including somatic delusions, are, of course, not accepted for brief psychotherapy because they lack insight into the psychological nature of their symptoms. Other problems can occur when the patient presents with a clear focus but the therapist feels that resolution of the focus will not provide adequate relief for the other psychopathology that is present but unrecognized by the patient. In this situation, the therapist will try to educate the patient as to the need for more extensive treatment. If this attempt fails, the therapist must decide whether or not to proceed with the brief treatment, recognizing the limited benefits for the patient. (Malan [1976a] has written on the use of brief psychotherapy in patients with severe psychopathology as well as the use of multiple foci in a single patient, but these treatments are not yet well established and are beyond the scope of this book.)

TECHNIQUE

There is an extensive literature on what factors are curative in psychotherapy, but, despite many years of study and controversy, there is still no general agreement on these matters. Most of the factors operating in long-term psychotherapy are present in the brief therapy situation: the patient–therapist relationship, the opportunity for abreaction, the opportunity for insight, and the use of dreams, fantasies, associations, and the manifestations of the transference. While there are obvious quantitative differences in the time spent on these components in long-term and brief psychotherapy, the main qualitative differences are in the limitation of the patient's regression and in the virtual elimination of the working-through phase of treatment in brief psychotherapy. Most of the modifications of technique employed in brief psychotherapy serve to limit the patient's regression and dependence on the therapist and to prevent the development of a transference neurosis. Because the transference is controlled, it is possible to utilize manifestations of the transference and still end the treatment without difficulty in the allotted time frame.

THE ACTIVITY OF THE THERAPIST

It is striking to compare pages of written transcripts of long-term and brief therapy. While the former will show long productions by the patient interspersed with brief comments by the therapist, the brief therapy transcripts show almost equal productions by patient and therapist, both producing relatively brief material at each interchange. There is a rapid back and forth between patient and therapist, both participating actively. How is this brought about? First of all, this is the norm of human communication, and if the patient is not taught differently, as is the case in long-term therapy, this type of equal interaction will tend to occur. More importantly, the therapist intervenes constantly to keep the therapy on the focus. Either by directing the patient's attention back to the focus, or by interpreting deviations from the focus to the patient, the therapist does not allow the patient to digress from the issues at hand. This not only serves to keep the therapy focused, but it also prevents the development of regression which occurs when the patient freely associates and then pursues the associations regardless of where they go. The inactivity and the blank-screen aspect of the analyst promote regression. The activity of the brief therapist retards regression. Thus, keeping the patient within the focus can be seen to have two purposes: to concentrate the material on the issue to be dealt with and to prevent regression which would make termination difficult.

The activity of the therapist also brings a special tone to the therapeutic situation. By his or her activity the therapist shows an interest in the work at hand, and the properly selected patient will respond to this by an increase in motivation and interest in the treatment. In addition, the therapist brings to the situation a sense of confidence and optimism, symbolized by the time limitation, which indicates to the patient that the therapist feels that a great deal can be accomplished in a short period of time. At the same time, the therapist indicates that it is up to the patient to do most of the work. The therapist frequently makes comments which highlight the patient's responsibilities and is quick to intervene when the patient tries to sit back and let the therapist do the work. All these factors tend to heighten the tension and the emotional content of the patient–therapist interaction. When the tension becomes too high, the therapist will use more supportive techniques to help maintain the optimal level of tension.

THE TRANSFERENCE

In the optimum brief therapy the patient's feelings and attitudes toward the therapist can be used to show the patient his or her characteristic manner of relating to significant people in his or her current life, as well as to demonstrate how the patient reacted to significant people in the past, all this while preventing the development of the transference neurosis. The main technique for achieving these results is the *early* interpretation of transference manifestations. Just as free associations with few interpretations lead to regression, so the uninterpreted flow of feelings of the patient toward the therapist leads to the development of a transference neurosis (Macalpine 1950). The early interpretation of transference manifestations brings these phenomena under the scrutiny of the observing portion of the patient's ego, putting the patient on guard, so to speak, against the dangers of dependency and regression which lie ahead. In this way the transference manifestations can be used in the therapy in a more controlled manner.

While the various authors differ on the details, in general both positive and negative transference phenomena are dealt with. However, not all transference manifestations which the therapist notes are interpreted. Transference, when used as a resistance, is always interpreted. Otherwise, transference interpretations are kept to the area of the focus. Within the focus, the patient's reaction to the therapist can be used to show his or her characteristic methods of defense, as well as to recreate some of the characteristic patterns which had been used with people from his or her past. Characterological responses to the therapist outside the area of the focus are generally not interpreted. Again, the limiting of the transference interpretations to the area of the focus tends to minimize regression and dependence on the therapist.

SETTING THE TIME FRAME

Treatment is conducted with the patient sitting up, face-to-face with the therapist, usually on a once-a-week basis. Sessions are 45 or 50 minutes in length. The face-to-face position promotes a sense of equality with the therapist and also, of course, tends to prevent regression. Little work has been done on varying the frequency of the visits, but it is probable that once-a-week sessions are optimal. More frequent sessions will tend to intensify the transference and will, therefore, complicate the termination process. Alexander and French (1946) have noted that a weekly interval allows the tension of the symptoms to build and at the same time encourages the patient to work on his or her own problems in the interval between sessions, thus diminishing the patient's dependence on the therapist.

Once the evaluation period has ended, which, as has been indicated, is extensive enough to gather a complete history and make a psychodynamic formulation, the patient is told that the therapy will be a brief one. The authors differ on the question of setting a definite time limit and on the length of the treatment, but all agree that the patient must be told in some way of the time frame before the treatment begins. (The therapies discussed in this book range from 5 to 40 sessions with the vast majority lasting from 12 to 30 sessions.) The knowledge that the treatment will be finite and limited has a profound effect on the course of the therapy. The patient knows there is little time to waste, and this encourages him or her to work hard in the therapy. At the same time the patient knows that the treatment will end in a fairly short period of time, and this allays fears of becoming excessively dependent on the treatment and on the therapist. Because of this, the patient is more likely to produce deep material during the time period of the brief therapy than in a comparable period at the beginning of an open-ended, long-term therapy. It is the general experience of therapists doing brief psychotherapy that brief therapy is a richer, more affect-laden experience for both patient and therapist than other types of therapy.

The role of the therapist in the course of the actual treatment varies among the different techniques. As noted, the therapist is active, but this does not mean that he or she is directive or needs to give up his or her usual therapeutic neutrality or reveal personal information. The task is for the patient to work psychotherapeutically within the focus. Resistance is dealt with; the specifics again vary with the technique. The patient's productions, associations, fantasies, slips, and dreams are utilized as in long-term therapy, although, of course, with less attention to detail and only when the material stays within the focus. Past history and memories are uncovered to shed light on the genesis of the current conflicts. An attempt is made to establish the "triangle of insight," that is, to interpret the conflict with its impulses and defenses as manifested in the patient's current life situation, in the transference, and in his or her past. There is no limitation on the depth at which the work can be carried out, only that it must be justified by the material which the patient has produced. Confirmation of interpretations occurs as it does in long-term therapy, with the production of new material, the release of affect, and changes in the patient's behavior within the therapy and in his or her actual life situation.

The authors discussed in the following chapters differ as to their criteria and techniques for termination. In general, when loss has been a significant aspect of the focus, this will be repeated in the transference at the time of termination and needs to be worked with. When the focus is an oedipal one, termination issues are often less important and require less attention from the therapist. Mann (1973), in contrast to the other workers, has made termination a central part of his particular treatment technique.

WORKING THROUGH

In long-term psychotherapy, once the basic conflict and the major defenses are elucidated, the ongoing work of the treatment generally consists of pointing out to the patient how that conflict and its defenses are manifested in the various aspects of the patient's life both within and outside the transference. This process of repeating and deepening interpretations as the conflict shows itself in many diverse areas is known as working through. It is not an error of organization that this discussion of working through in brief psychotherapy follows a discussion on termination, for in brief psychotherapy most of the process that is analogous to the working through of long-term psychotherapy takes place after the treatment has ended. While there may be time for some limited working through in the period after the conflicts have been understood and before the treatment ends, this is often not the case. How can treatment be effective without adequate working through? There are two main explanations for the effectiveness of brief therapy without this aspect of the treatment which heretofore was thought to be essential. One answer, most clearly stated by Wolberg (1980), is that the patient continues working through his or her conflicts after the treatment has ended. The patient takes the lessons which have been learned in the course of treatment and applies them to real life situations as they develop, thus continuing the process of therapy indefinitely. From this point of view brief therapy is as long as any psychoanalysis.

The other explanation for the success of brief therapy without working through depends on the concept that small changes produce positive feedback which in turn leads to further changes. Thus, after termination, the patient, because of the changes achieved in the therapy, will interact with the people in his or her environment in a different way, and they in turn will react to him or her differently. Through this feedback loop, positive changes are reinforced and lead to further positive changes. Marmor (1979) has pointed out that the original analytic theorists saw the mind as a closed system, so that unless all aspects of a conflict were treated, symptom relief in one area would lead to an emergence of symptoms in another area. By seeing the individual as an open system, reacting with his or her environment, symptom substitution no longer becomes a necessity. Thus, symptom relief could lead to a more positive interaction with others, resulting in reinforcement of the patient's changed behavior.

Symptoms are always a compromise, and the idea that brief treatment can bring about change implies that the forces involved in the symptom formation are in relatively close balance, so that a small shift in the balance of those forces can lead to major changes. To a distant observer a seesaw with a 1-pound weight on one side and a 99-pound weight on the other will look identical to a seesaw with a 49-pound weight on one side and a 51-pound weight on the other, but the amount of force required to shift the seesaw's position will obviously vary greatly in the two examples. So, too, a symptom that is heavily invested by the patient will be hard to change. For example, a patient may present with a symptom of obesity about which he or she complains relatively little. History reveals that the patient uses the obesity to remain home with his or her parents, avoiding all social and sexual contacts, and blaming a lack of vocational success on the weight problem. It is obvious that such a symptom would not respond to a brief intervention. All symptoms are overdetermined, and brief treatment can only address the major determinants. For this reason, symptom relief is usually not complete after brief therapy; rather, there is an amelioration in the intensity of the symptom and the importance which it plays in the patient's life.

PROBLEMS FOR THE THERAPIST

For therapists experienced only in long-term therapy, a common problem is seeing brief therapy as second best. For at least the past 50 years, there has been a generally accepted hierarchy in psychotherapy: psychoanalysis is the best form of treatment available, long-term psychotherapy has merit if psychoanalysis is not possible, and lesser forms of therapy are makeshift at best. There is a similar hierarchy for therapists, with psychoanalysts having the highest status. These general values are inconsistent with the optimism and confidence that the brief therapist must have in the method and which must be brought to the treatment situation. Problems will therefore arise if the therapist undertakes brief therapy because it is required by his or her training program or job. The patient approaches the treatment with ambivalence. In brief therapy much of this ambivalence focuses on the question "Can I be helped in such a short time?" If the therapist shares this ambivalence, the treatment is not likely to succeed. Sifneos (1979) found that teaching his method of brief psychotherapy to volunteers only was much more successful than when he attempted to teach it to all members of his department's training program, and the same phenomenon would undoubtedly be observed with other methods of brief therapy. A therapist should, therefore, not attempt to treat a patient with brief therapy unless he or she really believes that the goals of the treatment can be met with that particular form of therapy. For a student, this sense of conviction is of course impossible. What is required of a student is an open mind, a willingness to try the method, and an ability to put aside previously acquired prejudices about length of treatment.

On the other hand, problems will arise if the brief therapist is too zealous about his or her methods. In an attempt to show how useful brief therapy is, it is possible to overlook contraindications and take patients into brief treatment who would have been better served with other modalities. Once the treatment has begun, the therapist may pervert his or her activity into a struggle for control, insisting that his or her formulations are correct and not really listening to the patient's material. Without careful attention to the data, strict adherence to making interpretations only when the data warrant them, and looking for appropriate confirmations before proceeding, brief therapy can become a "wild analysis," which may satisfy some of the needs of the therapist to show how good he or she is at making an interpretation, but will surely not benefit the patient. Similarly, the therapist with a need to be controlling can misuse the role to become overly directive and manipulative in the patient's actual life situations, turning the treatment from a psychotherapeutic one into authoritarian advice giving. More common is the therapist who is so afraid of becoming too controlling that he or she is not active enough in the therapy and allows it to drift away from the focus.

For therapists working in an institutional setting the status of having a "long-term case" may make them overlook the benefits of brief therapy in a given situation. For those working in a private practice there is a monetary factor in addition to the issue of status. It is difficult, when confronted with a patient who can pay the therapist's fees and who can clearly benefit from twice-a-week psychotherapy which will probably last two or three years, to recommend a course of brief therapy which will yield the therapist 10 percent of the income of the long-term treatment. Particularly in areas where there is no shortage of therapists, the economic factor can be an important source of bias in the treatment selection, although this is usually not conscious with the therapist.

TEACHING BRIEF PSYCHOTHERAPY

At the present time, there is a paradox in the teaching of brief psychotherapy. Ideally, the student coming to learn brief therapy should have the knowledge and skills acquired from many years of experience with long-term therapy while not having become habituated to any of his or her own techniques. The brief therapist is required to achieve a correct diagnosis and psychodynamic formulation within the initial interviews. He or she is required to select an accurate focus and keep the patient working within that focus, modifying it when necessary. The therapist must be able to tell which of the patient's productions fall within the focus and which are resistances or extraneous, and he or she must make the appropriate interpretations, including transference interpretations, keeping the level of tension in the treatment high, while not allowing unnecessary regression to occur. The therapist must conduct the treatment in such a manner that the goals can be achieved and a satisfactory termination occurs. All of this must be done within the agreed-upon time frame. When looked at like this, it is clear why years of experience with psychotherapy would be helpful. But, at the same time, the techniques and attitudes learned during those years, the listening with free-floating attention, the encouragement of the patient's associations, the interest in *all* of the patient's productions, the sense of timelessness, that what won't be dealt with today will be dealt with the next time, the limitation of interventions by the therapist, all these and more must be put in abeyance.

In some ways it is easier to teach brief therapy to a novice in psychotherapy, because he or she has much less to unlearn. In that case, however, strict supervision is required, particularly in the selection process, lest inappropriate patients be treated. There should be at least one hour of supervision for each treatment hour, and the process notes should be carefully studied. It is useful to train the student from the beginning to prepare before each hour by recalling what has occurred before and anticipating what will take place in the forthcoming session. The anticipation should, of course, never become a treatment "plan," for each session must depend on what the patient brings up, not on what the therapist would like the patient to bring up.

Brief psychotherapy is often a helpful addition to the middle portion of a training program. During this phase of training, the trainee has acquired enough psychotherapeutic skill to be an enthusiastic practitioner, but frequently becomes discouraged because the usual teaching cases, that is, long-term therapy patients, do not readily display the phenomena about which the trainee has read and wants to experience for himself or herself. Because brief therapy condenses what happens in the treatment, the trainee can soon observe changes in resistance, shifting defenses, responses to correct interpretations, and a whole range of transference phenomena, as well as seeing symptom amelioration and changes in the patient's life situation. The effect on the trainee is often similar to the effect that good therapy has on a patient—an affectual awareness of what had heretofore been only an intellectual concept ("I've read about these things, but now I *know* they're true").

At the other end of the spectrum the experienced therapist learning brief psychotherapy also needs careful supervision. He or she will need less help with the diagnosis and psychodynamics, but will need continuous surveillance lest long-term techniques creep into the therapy. Here again, careful process notes are essential. The factors discussed in the previous section on countertransference all apply to students of brief therapy and must be considered in their training.

BRIEF THERAPY—A TREATMENT OF CHOICE?

Some writers (e.g., Shafer 1973) will grant that benefits can come from a course of brief psychotherapy but will say that it is always second best to long-term treatment; that is, no one who is realistically able to have long-term treatment should have brief treatment. Others, of course, state that brief psychotherapy is often the treatment of choice, regardless of what other forms of therapy are available. Assuming a clinical situation where a patient meets the criteria for a method of brief psychotherapy and has the time and the means for long-term therapy, what are the advantages and disadvantages of choosing the brief approach? There are benefits to the patient in savings of both time and money. (If a patient is healthy enough to qualify for brief therapy, there will surely be other things for him or her to spend time and money on.) But, more importantly, being in treatment is itself a statement to the patient, a statement that he or she is "not well," "needs help," and that some time in the future, after the treatment has ended, he or she will be better able to accomplish life goals than while still in treatment. These factors combine to diminish the patient's self-esteem, increase dependency on the therapist, and cause the patient to procrastinate in regard to actually living his or her life. Alexander and French (1946) have emphasized that often the gratification of dependency in the treatment situation outweighs the pain of the symptoms, causing treatment to be prolonged indefinitely. Similarly, an indefinite termination date allows the patient to put off facing the issue of separation from the therapist indefinitely, and in this way he or she can postpone dealing with certain aspects of reality (see Mann, Chapter 5). At its most extreme, a prolonged treatment situation can become the main interest of the patient's life. As has been noted, a treatment with a definite time frame does not permit this type of dependency and procrastination, and implicitly and explicitly encourages the patient to work on the particular problem so he or she can get on to living his or her life. It is true that in brief therapy there are always issues left unresolved, but unless there are clear indications that these issues interfere seriously with the patient's feeling or functioning, long-term therapy does not seem indicated.

The issues described in the previous paragraph are particularly significant for patients in late adolescence and early adulthood. At this age, the individual is usually struggling with issues of independence and dependence. Brief therapy avoids dependency and permits the patient to proceed to age-appropriate tasks, while long-term therapy in this age group, unless clearly indicated, can have the effect of stultifying the normal maturational processes.

There is another group of patients for whom long-term treatment might be indicated, but who resist it for various reasons. This group includes those people who, because of their cultural upbringing, are suspicious of psychotherapy. Many people believe that psychotherapy is only for the "crazy," that the therapist is able to "control your mind," and that the therapist will change your values to his or her own. As noted by Mann (1973), people who fear open-ended treatment for these reasons are more likely to accept a brief therapy, realizing that they will have better control over the situation if the termination date is known in advance.

Similarly, some individuals who are frightened of their unconscious feelings, fantasies, and impulses, who fear discovering what "craziness" or "badness" lies inside them, and who fear loss of control of their impulses should they become aware of them will accept brief therapy while resisting long-term treatment. This is particularly true of people who are frightened of their unacceptable dependency wishes. People in middle or late life who have, in a sense, made peace with their neurosis and who do not wish to explore the major conflicts of their life also will often accept brief therapy directed to one particular focus that is currently paining them.

At this time it is not known what percentage of people seeking psychotherapy are suitable for brief therapy. The various techniques have separate selection criteria, and clinics serve different populations, so that meaningful statistics are difficult to collect. As more therapists are trained in these techniques, more and more patients will be treated with brief psychotherapy. When the public at large becomes aware that there is substantial benefit available from these techniques, many people will come to seek help who now avoid it because of the commitment of time and money required and, more importantly, because of the fear of dependency and loss of control engendered by open-ended psychotherapy.

2

THE HISTORY OF ANALYTICALLY ORIENTED BRIEF PSYCHOTHERAPY

BREUER AND FREUD—*STUDIES ON HYSTERIA* (1895)

Psychoanalysis grew out of the cathartic method described by Breuer and Freud in their *Studies on Hysteria*. Many of the elements which today characterize analytically oriented brief psychotherapy can be traced back to that work. Subsequently the development of brief psychotherapy and the development of psychoanalysis were intertwined in such a way that most major attempts at promoting brief psychotherapy were seen by Freud and his followers as attempts to modify and undermine the basic principles of psychoanalysis and thus to destroy psychoanalysis as they understood it. Because Freud's preeminent interest was psychoanalysis, many of the discoveries first presented in *Studies on Hysteria* were not utilized in any systematic manner until the reemergence of brief psychotherapy during the last 25 years.

Breuer and Freud believed that symptoms were caused by the repression of traumatic memories and their accompanying affects. If these memories could be brought into consciousness and the affects experienced and discharged, the symptoms would abate. The aim of their treatment was to get the patient to remember the traumatic event which first led to the formation of symptoms. In the original patient treated by Breuer, Anna O., Breuer used hypnosis to allow the patient to overcome her resistances and remember the origins of her various symptoms. In later cases, all treated by Freud, hypnosis was used at times. However, Freud, noting that all patients could not be hypnotized, developed his concentration technique which consisted of the patient lying on a couch with eyes closed while Freud applied pressure on the forehead from time to time to help the patient concentrate on remembering the events surrounding the origin of the symptom. By means of the patient's efforts and the therapist's urgings, the lost memories and affects were recovered. Later Freud stopped applying pressure to the forehead and urged the patient to remember without any physical contact.

Of the cases described in the *Studies*, only Lucy R. fits into the time frame that today constitutes brief psychotherapy. She was seen approximately once a week for nine weeks, but no infantile traumata were involved in the clearing of her symptoms. Katerina was seen by Freud on only one occasion. The other patients were seen usually in daily visits; Emmy von N. for seven weeks during her first year of treatment and for eight weeks in her second year of treatment, Anna O. for about 18 months, and no time of treatment is given for Elisabeth von R., although the treatment was not brief. Freud was developing a new technique for treating a serious condition which heretofore had resisted all available treatment modalities, and he was not concerned with the problem of how long the therapy would last—any successful therapy, regardless of length, would be an important contribution. Nevertheless, many of the techniques Freud employed in the cathartic method are now part of the techniques of brief psychotherapy.

While Freud's original selection criteria are not as well defined as today's selection criteria for brief therapy, he does say that the cathartic method is not for everyone, and he does list some selection criteria. The patient should have a "certain level of intelligence." The patient should have confidence in the procedure; that is, he or she must begin the treatment with a positive attitude toward the therapist and the particular mode of therapy, and he or she should show a high level of motivation so that the patient can overcome the resistance which will be aroused when he or she sees "the direction in which the treatment is going," that is, the sexual origins of the neurosis (p. 265).

Freud advocates a great deal of activity for the therapist. The therapist must have confidence in his or her technique and that confidence must be conveyed to the patient. The therapist frequently insists that the patient can produce a thought or a memory relevant to the topic being explored. The flow of the material is encouraged by the use of pressure on the patient's forehead. When there is resistance the therapist will often attack it directly. The following fragment from the treatment of Lucy R. illustrates some of these points. The tone is quite similar to that which Sifneos uses today (see Chapter 4).

To begin with she only knew that this first attack came over her while she was out shopping in the principal street.

TH: What were you going to buy?
PT: Different things, I believe; they were for a ball I had been invited to.
TH: When was this ball to take place?
PT: Two days later, I think.
TH: Something must have happened to agitate you a few days before, something that made an impression on you.
PT: I can't think of anything. After all, it was twenty-one years ago.
TH: That makes no difference; you will remember all the same. I shall press your head, and when I relax the pressure, you will think of something or see something, and you must tell me what that is.

I went through this procedure; but she remained silent.

TH: Well, has nothing occurred to you?
PT: I have thought of something, but it can't have any connection with this.
TH: Tell it to me anyway.

PT: I thought of a friend of mine, a girl, who is dead. But she died when I was eighteen—a year later, that is.

TH: We shall see. Let's stick to this point. What about this friend of yours?

PT: Her death was a great shock to me, as I used to see a lot of her. A few weeks earlier another girl had died, and that had made a great stir in the town. So, after all, I must have been seventeen at the time.

TH: There, you see, I told you we could rely on the things that come into your head under the pressure of my hand. Now, can you remember what you were thinking about when you felt dizzy in the street.

PT: I wasn't thinking of anything; I only felt dizzy.

TH: That's not possible. States like that never happen without being accompanied by some idea. I shall press once more and the thought you had will come back to you. . . . Well, what has occurred to you?

PT: The idea that I am the third.

TH: What does that mean?

PT: When I got the attack of dizziness I must have thought: "Now I am dying, like the other two girls."

TH: That was the idea, then. As you were having the attack you thought of your friend. So her death must have made a great impression on you.

PT: Yes, it did. I can remember now that when I heard of her death I felt it was dreadful to be going to a ball, while she was dead. But I was looking forward so much to the ball and was so busy with preparations for it; I didn't want to think of what had happened at all. (p. 113)

In addition to confronting the patient and insisting that the patient can produce relevant material, the therapist is also supportive and educational, informing the patient of the workings of the mind and getting the patient to participate in the treatment as a collaborator, thus undoing some of the dependency incurred by the authoritative stance of the therapist. In addition, Breuer and Freud were already aware of some aspects of the concept of transference and stated that transference could be utilized in the treatment, although they do not emphasize this aspect of the treatment. Indeed, they state that material may be considered *either* in the transference or in the memories of past events.

> For the patient the work remained the same: she had to overcome the distressing affect aroused by having been able to entertain such a wish even for a moment; and it seemed to make no difference to the success of the treatment whether she made this psychical repudiation the theme of her work in the historical instance or in the recent one connected with me. (p. 304)

It is only later that the transference becomes the essential element in the therapy.

While a focus as such is not mentioned in the *Studies on Hysteria*, the technique consisted of following only those ideas which occurred to the patient in relation to each symptom. Each symptom was thus analyzed until its traumatic origins were elucidated and the appropriate affect experienced. By concentrating on the connections to a specific symptom, other thoughts were excluded, and the effect was to limit the treatment to a circumscribed set of associations. No characterological issues were dealt with. Little attention was paid to what was later called working through or to issues of termination.

Thus some of the essential elements of brief psychotherapy—selection on the basis of intelligence and motivation; activity by the therapist involving confrontation and support; and limitation of the treatment to a circumscribed area—can be seen in the *Studies on Hysteria*. The cathartic method also, of course, differs in important ways from brief psychotherapy today. Freud did not set a time limit or indicate to the patient that the therapy would be brief. He did not select patients on the basis of their psychological health. Indeed, most of Freud's early patients were severely ill people who had proven refractory to other forms of treatment and came to Freud after other physicians had failed to provide relief of their symptoms. For the same reason, Freud did not select patients on the basis of the focality of their symptoms. Although he was aware of transference manifestations, he did not use transference interpretations extensively, in contrast to the brief therapy techniques of today. Also, at the time of writing the *Studies*, he had not yet developed the interpretation of defenses and the use of dreams and fantasies.

Freud soon repudiated his cathartic method. In *A Case of Hysteria* (1905) he writes that since *Studies on Hysteria*

"psycho-analytic technique has been completely revolution-
ized" (p. 12). He then describes the technique of free association and says that this new technique is much superior to the
older one of following the associations back from the symptoms. "Indeed there can be no doubt that it [the new tech-
nique] can be the only possible one" (p. 12). This statement of
Freud's lays the foundation for the subsequent resistance to
brief psychotherapy. In trying to develop psychoanalysis,
Freud discarded his cathartic technique and never pursued it
to fully determine its usefulness or limitations. He was not
interested in forms of psychotherapy other than psychoanalysis, and, indeed, he saw any deviation from psychoanalysis as
a threat to psychoanalysis itself. As psychoanalysis developed,
therapy took longer and longer and bore less and less resem-
blance to brief psychotherapy as we know it today. The
activity of the therapist declined; he or she became less
challenging and less supportive; and the utilization of free
associations eliminated the focusing of the treatment on only
one aspect of the patient's mental productions.

These changes followed inevitably from the technique of
free association. An active therapist is incompatible with a
free-associating patient (although with Dora, in *A Case of
Hysteria*, Freud was still quite active). The more the therapist
talks, the more he or she interrupts the patient's associations,
so that Freud's "new technique" led to the increasing inactivity and passivity of the therapist. The result of the combination of the patient's free associations and the therapist's passivity was a deepening regression leading to the formation of
the transference neurosis, which required time to analyze
once it was formed. When it was recognized that the transference neurosis was the main therapeutic tool, those factors
which tended to help form the transference neurosis were, of
course, encouraged. Malan (1963) has reviewed these and
other factors leading to the lengthening of psychoanalytic
therapy. He notes that the analysis of resistances added considerably to the length of the therapy. Later, with the emergence of ego psychology and the analysis of defenses and
character traits, additional time was required. The early therapies did not include much working through, and when it
became evident that this was often required, the treatment
again became longer. With the formation of a transference
neurosis in the patient, termination became much more of an

issue, and, indeed, there was often great resistance shown by the patient toward ending the treatment, and this too had to be analyzed. Malan points out that there were also changes in the analyst that contributed to the longer treatments. As part of the therapeutic neutrality the analyst often developed a sense of timelessness which was conveyed to the patient; so both parties in the analysis felt that it could go on indefinitely until all issues were resolved. The analyst became more and more perfectionistic, looking to analyze all aspects of the patient's psychic life and hoping to trace back all conflicts to as early a developmental level as was possible. This all required time.

Malan also reviews "analytic" cases which were published by therapists other than Freud before 1914. These treatments were often relatively brief and successful. He notes that many of these therapies still followed the cathartic method. A review of his sources reveals a varying mixture of cathartic and analytic techniques which were being carried on long after Freud had abandoned all elements of the cathartic method in his own work. The work of these early therapists is characterized by the kind of drama and enthusiasm which is seen in much of today's brief therapy. In addition, there was much attention paid to "complexes," which were groups of associations, memories, and affects organized around a particular traumatic event, usually in childhood. The aim of the therapy was often to follow the associations of the complex until all aspects of the complex could be made conscious. By concentrating on the analysis of the complexes, these early therapies were practicing focal therapy, although the term was not used at that time.

The early case material which was published is limited, and it is not clear how much of this type of therapy was actually being practiced between 1895 and 1914. There is much anecdotal material about the early brief and successful therapies (e.g., Ferenczi and Rank 1925), but little hard data. What is clear is that this type of case material ceases to appear in the analytic, that is, Freudian, literature after 1914. Brief psychotherapies that developed outside the mainstream of classical psychoanalysis, such as the work of Stekel, will not be considered in this chapter. As will be seen in the subsequent sections, the current models of brief psychotherapy which are the subject of this book grew directly out of the work of Freud and his followers.

FERENCZI AND RANK—*THE DEVELOPMENT OF PSYCHOANALYSIS* (1923)

Ferenczi and Rank were the first major writers to address the issue of the lengthening treatments. Their book *The Development of Psychoanalysis* was written in 1922 and published in German in 1923 and in English translation in 1925. The book is a difficult one to read. It is written by two authors who do not always seem to agree with one another. The language used is quite out of date, and there are no case examples given to clarify the points made. In addition, it could be speculated that the authors were trying to be circumspect in presenting their ideas so as not to run counter to the main tenets of Freud's psychoanalysis. In spite of this, it is possible to see in this work important precursors of present-day brief psychotherapy.

While Freud (1937) had used a fixed time limit for his therapy with the Wolf-Man and other cases, Rank (Ferenczi and Rank 1925) was the first to advocate using a fixed time limit as part of general analytic treatment. He felt that after the transference neurosis had formed, the therapist should set a definite time limit for the ending of the therapy and that it should be strictly adhered to; the rationale being that during the initial phase of the treatment the patient's fantasies are mobilized and gratified in the transference situation. Setting a time limit forces the patient to face reality and learn to give up the unrealistic aspects of his or her fantasies. This clearly anticipates Mann (see Chapter 5) and the phases of therapy he describes as resulting from the setting of a fixed time limit (see also Marmor 1979 for a discussion of the relationship of Mann and Rank).

While Rank is associated with the development of the time limit, Ferenczi is known for advocating "active" therapy. In a series of papers from 1919 to 1925, Ferenczi (1952) noted that there were limitations to the technique of free association and that at times specific commands should be given to the patient, either to engage in or to desist from certain activities. He emphasizes that these active techniques are the exception to the rule of free association and should be used rarely and only when clearly indicated, for example, as a means of combating the intellectualizing of a severely obsessional patient.

In taking this position he did not differ significantly from positions taken by Freud.

In *The Development of Psychoanalysis*, however, Ferenczi and Rank describe a much broader role for the active therapist than was noted in the above-cited papers. They state that psychoanalysis often becomes overly intellectual and posit this is often a result of mixing up the investigative and therapeutic aspects of psychoanalysis. As a research tool, psychoanalysis is indispensible for exploring the development of the mind, but often analysts, in their desire to corroborate their theory with each patient, undertake a complete analysis when this is not necessary. Ferenczi and Rank emphasize that "in the correctly executed analysis the whole development of the individual is not repeated, but only those phases of development of the infantile libido on which the ego . . . has remained fixed" (p. 19). When the therapy goes deeper than is necessary, the treatment becomes too intellectual for the patient because he or she no longer is that emotionally invested in the problems that arise. Intellectual knowledge without affect serves as a resistance. The therapist, therefore, must be active to maintain the therapy at the proper level and to avoid associations that go beyond this level. (This is related to maintaining a focus.) The therapist must also be active in order to maintain the proper emotional tension throughout the treatment.

Ferenczi and Rank state that change comes about through the patient's experiencing the affects as well as the intellectual understanding of the original, usually oedipal, conflict in the transference. To evoke the necessary affect, which they say is achieved with the cathartic method but often not experienced through free associations alone, the therapist must at times be active to "provoke" the affects, whether by direct commands or prohibitions, or by assuming a transference stance which is fitted to the needs of the patient and which will elicit the desired affect. (Here they anticipate Alexander and French's "manipulation" of the transference [see Chapter 3].)

Thus, one can see in *The Development of Psychoanalysis* three of the main elements of brief psychotherapy, albeit in rough form—the time limit, the focus, and the active therapist keeping the emotional tension high. The factors that caused this material to be generally ignored for 20 years until it was reformulated by Alexander and French are complicated, involving, among other things, the personalities of Ferenczi and Rank and their relationship to Freud and his other close associates, as well as Freud's need to maintain the integrity of the psychoanalytic movement (Jones 1957). Insofar as Ferenczi and Rank did not present their work as an alternate form of therapy suitable for some patients, but rather as a general substitute for psychoanalysis, they might have anticipated the criticism that followed. Freud was initially ambivalent in his reaction to Rank's concept of a fixed time limit in psychoanalysis. He felt it was not generally useful and hoped that Rank would discover this for himself. (Ferenczi did in fact stop using a time limit in his own work.) Around this time Rank's ideas about therapy became connected with his belief that the birth trauma was the central issue in neurosis and that this was all that had to be analyzed. This concept, combined with the time limit, resulted in quite short treatments, often only three to four months long. In rejecting the Oedipus complex as central to the genesis of the neurosis, Rank took a position which Freud could not accept, and the two men ended their relationship in 1926.

Most of Ferenczi's contributions to brief therapy were also lost in controversy. During the late 1920s he became increasingly estranged from Freud, although they never terminated their friendship. His active therapy, while originally quite conservative, became more and more extreme, leading to physical contact between himself and his patients and to other attempts by him to directly gratify some of their previously unsatisfied needs. By the time of his death in 1933 Ferenczi had lost much of the influence he had previously had in the psychoanalytic community.

Freud (1937) commented on Rank's efforts to shorten therapy by limiting the analysis to the birth trauma and setting a time limit.

We have not heard much about what the implementation of Rank's plan has done for cases of sickness. Probably not more than if the fire-brigade, called to deal with a house that had been set on fire by an overturned oil-lamp, contented themselves with removing the lamp from the room in which the blaze had started. No doubt considerable shortening of the brigade's activity would be effected by this means. (pp. 216–217)

While Freud's criticism of Rank's work may well have been valid, Freud's metaphor reveals his position that psychoanalysis can be the only valid form of therapy.*

Freud practiced brief therapy himself. He treated Bruno Walter successfully for cramps in his conducting arm in a few visits in 1906 (Sterba 1951). The therapy consisted of a suggestion to take a vacation, and when the symptom was still present on Walter's return, Freud told him that he would gradually be able to conduct, and these latter suggestions did, indeed, work. How many brief suggestive treatments Freud engaged in is not known, because he never published any of them; the Bruno Walter therapy came to light only because Walter described it in his memoirs. Freud's training analyses were often brief; the early ones sometimes lasted only a few weeks, but Freud distinguished between training analyses and therapeutic analyses. It is not known how many brief therapeutic analyses Freud conducted.

Freud recognized no form of analytically oriented psychotherapy other than psychoanalysis. Even in his famous quote about alloying the pure gold of analysis with copper in order to be able to fulfill the anticipated large-scale demands for therapy (Freud 1919, p. 168), the copper refers to suggestion and hypnosis and not to such modifications of analytic technique as limiting free associations or choosing circumscribed foci and goals. This attitude on the part of Freud made it difficult for any of his followers to develop alternate forms of therapy. The semantics of the situation added to the difficulty. Psychoanalysis was the only word available to describe any therapy based on Freudian theory. Thus, Ferenczi and Rank called their book *The Development of Psycho-*

---

* Using a similar metaphor for brief psychotherapy, one could reply that, if, when the fire brigade enters the house, they find that the fire which has been started by the overturned oil-lamp is confined to the living room floor, then it may not always be necessary to open the walls in all the other rooms of the house in order to make sure that there are no hidden sparks there. No one technique of fire fighting suits all fires.

analysis. One could easily criticize their work and say "this is not psychoanalysis," meaning this is not the therapy that Freud has been teaching, while a defender of the book could just as easily say "this is psychoanalysis," meaning a form of therapy based on analytic principles and derived from Freud's work.

ALEXANDER AND FRENCH— *PSYCHOANALYTIC THERAPY* (1946)

In 1938, Franz Alexander, then head of the Chicago Institute for Psychoanalysis, began a research project to "define those basic principles which make possible a shorter and more efficient means of psychotherapy, and whenever possible to develop specific means of treatment" (Alexander and French 1946, p. iii). As part of this project, members of the Chicago Institute treated nearly 600 patients at both the Institute and in private practice. The results of this work were published by Alexander and French in 1946 in their book *Psychoanalytic Therapy.* The historical aspects of their work will be considered here, while the specifics of their technique will be discussed in the following chapter.

Alexander's* work is a direct continuation of the work of Ferenczi and Rank, as he himself acknowledges. He held a prestigious position in the psychoanalytic community and was able to bring his prestige and that of his Institute to bear on the question of modifying psychoanalysis. In contrast to Ferenczi and Rank, Alexander and French present their ideas in a clear and forceful manner, well documented with case material.

Alexander began by questioning the assumption that had governed Freud and his followers: that the depth of the therapy and the quality of therapeutic results are *necessarily* proportionate to the length of the treatment and to the frequency of the interviews. (As will be seen below, this is an excellent statement of what Malan [1976a] calls the "radical view" of brief psychotherapy.) Once this assumption is questioned, the development of alternate, briefer techniques becomes pos-

---

* Alexander is generally credited with being the chief contributor to the ideas of his group, even though the book is coauthored with French.

sible. In certain circumstances, these new techniques may be as efficacious as classical analysis. Indeed, Alexander goes further and states that some of the alternative techniques may often be superior to psychoanalysis in that psychoanalysis often perpetuates the patient's regression. The gratification the patient receives from the regression, hence from the treatment, can lead to unnecessarily prolonged treatment.

Much of what Alexander advocates is designed to minimize regression. Like Ferenczi and Rank he argues that it is not necessary to analyze all aspects of every patient's mental life. The analysis need only go back to the point at which the trauma which caused the present difficulty occurred. Any probing beyond (i.e., developmentally earlier than) that point is not therapeutic, but only leads to nonproductive regression. Such technical devices as varying the frequency of the sessions, interrupting the treatment, and using the chair instead of the couch are used to help minimize the regression.

Each patient, after an initial evaluation, should have a specific individual treatment plan devised on the basis of as complete a psychodynamic understanding of the patient as is possible. Included in the evaluation are not only such factors as the developmental phase to which the symptoms can be traced and the type of resistances that the patient shows, but also the ego-strengths of the patient, for the length of the therapy will depend very much on these. Alexander states that the intensity of the treatment should be geared to the assessment of the ego of the patient. The stronger the patient's ego, the more the therapist will push the material, resulting in a briefer and more intense therapy. While some of the cases described by Alexander are quite brief, he does not set a time limit, nor does he tell the patient that the therapy will be a brief one.

The therapist is active in order to minimize regression and to keep the emotional tension high throughout the treatment. Like Ferenczi and Rank, Alexander believes in the importance of the emotional component of the therapy. Indeed, he believes that what he calls the corrective emotional experience is essential to effecting change in any treatment. The corrective emotional experience is the reliving by the patient of the original traumatic experience in relation to the therapist or to some other person in his or her life, this time with a more favorable resolution than in the original childhood conflict. By recognizing that the corrective emotional experience can occur outside of the transference to the therapist, Alexander eliminates the need for the transference to be used therapeutically within each treatment situation. He returns here to ideas first formulated by Breuer and Freud in *Studies on Hysteria.* Alexander advocates that the therapist "manipulate" the transference, that is, assume a role that will most readily evoke the corrective emotional experience. Here Alexander follows ideas first presented by Ferenczi and Rank.

Today, many of Alexander's ideas seem commonplace, and many of them have been adopted by therapists practicing analytically oriented psychotherapy, but at the time his contributions were quite controversial, so that some aspects of his technique have never been generally accepted: for example, his ideas concerning trial interruptions, and especially the manipulation of the transference. His theory of the corrective emotional experience is also generally not given the central place in the theory of change that it had for Alexander. Another source of controversy was a result of Alexander's method of presenting his ideas. Again, as with Ferenczi and Rank, the distinction between psychotherapy and psychoanalysis became blurred. By 1946, the semantic confusion noted above no longer was prevalent, and psychoanalysis and analytically oriented psychotherapy were generally understood to be two separate if related modalities of treatment, even if the boundaries between them were not clearly delineated. Alexander is well aware of the distinction and refers to the classical analytic technique as "the standard technique." He sees the standard technique as one variant of psychoanalytic therapy. While Alexander acknowledges that the standard technique might be useful for chronic neurosis (in another place [Alexander 1944] he wrote that he "rarely" treated anyone with the standard technique anymore), his general tone throughout the book is one of condescension for an inferior technique, quite similar in tone to that used by Freud and his followers when discussing therapies other than psychoanalysis. Thus, many critics responded to Alexander's book as though it were an attack on psychoanalysis. Once again, the main issue became one of defending Freud and classical psychoanalysis against any encroachment, and in this process the many valuable contributions of Alexander tended to be overlooked.

Despite the criticism, the impact of Alexander's work was enormous, although the influence of the book was exerted

through somewhat unofficial channels. Little of relevance appeared in the psychiatric or psychoanalytic literature in the
years following the publication of the book. However, as
noted by Marmor (1979), ideas promulgated by Alexander
became part of the armamentarium of most practicing therapists. Interestingly, Alexander influenced long-term analytically oriented psychotherapy almost immediately, but he
had little influence on brief therapy for nearly 20 years, even
though his case material contains many brief cases, and much
of what he wrote has direct application to brief therapy techniques. It is not clear why this should be so. Probably the jump
from psychoanalysis to brief therapy was too great to be
made in one leap, and it was necessary for analytically oriented long-term therapy to be established as a legitimate and
effective modality of treatment before further modifications
could be entertained by the profession.

OTHER WORK (1936–1970)

Malan (1963, 1976a) has reviewed the brief therapy literature of this period. The published material consists of isolated
case reports or reports of small series of patients treated with a
variety of brief techniques with little attempt by the authors at
formulating any specific system of brief therapy. Malan divided the papers into two groups, the "conservative" and the
"radical." The conservative position is that brief therapy is of
benefit, but only in limited situations. The patients for whom
it is suited are those with good ego-strengths, that is, healthy
patients who have no history of serious difficulties either in
regard to functioning or to previous symptom formation. The
symptoms that can be treated by brief techniques must be of
recent onset and should be relatively mild. The conservative
technique consists of making interpretations that are limited
to the patient's current reality situation, and interpretations
involving the transference or the patient's childhood relationships are avoided. The goal of the treatment is the reestablish-
ment of the patient's previous level of functioning.

The radical position is that brief therapy can benefit a
wider variety of patients. Symptoms need not be of recent
origin, and they can be quite incapacitating. The radical technique involves the full range of psychotherapeutic techniques,
including transference interpretations and recovery of mate-

rial relating to early childhood. The goal of the therapy is not only symptom removal but also may include some characterological changes and improved functioning compared to the premorbid condition of the patient. The therapies described in this book all follow the radical position.

Malan concludes from his review of the literature that while there is evidence that the conservative view is valid, that is, healthy patients with mild acute psychopathology can be helped with brief interventions of a relatively superficial nature, this view is not the only correct one. There is evidence that the radical position can be valid, namely, that some relatively sick patients with long-standing psychopathology can be helped with brief interventions that go quite deep. Malan emphasizes, as did Alexander before him, that the radical position does not invalidate the conservative one and that deep interpretations and transference interpretations are not always needed to bring about the desired results.

The work of Felix Deutsch deserves special mention. He developed what he called "sector therapy," which entailed restricting the therapy to "a limited area of the patient's intrapsychic life and confining one's efforts to a thorough exploration of one aspect of a recurrent problem within this area" (Deutsch and Murphy, vol. 2, p. 124). While Ferenczi and Rank and Alexander had written about selecting specific aspects of the patient's conflict and dealing only with those, they did not give this aspect of their work particular prominence. But Deutsch made the selection and maintenance of the sector the most important part of his technique. He thus emphasized the issue of focality, which became so important in the methods of the later workers. Deutsch also developed the "associative anamnesis." Originally used in evaluation interviews, it later became an essential part of his technique of sector therapy. The technique consists of the therapist picking up on certain key words, affects, or behaviors of the patient and repeating them to the patient. The key words are selected on the basis of the therapist's psychodynamic understanding of the patient and are chosen because they reflect central aspects of the patient's conflicts. By thus speaking directly to the patient's unconscious, the therapeutic alliance is strengthened, and the patient feels understood more rapidly than by using standard techniques. It also serves to keep the treatment focused. Sector therapy can be considered a mixed therapy on the radical–conservative spectrum; it is radical in that it seeks to uncover unconscious material in relation to long-standing conflicts, but conservative in that it uses transference interpretations minimally. Deutsch does not emphasize the brevity of his treatment—he sets no time limit and his treatments are of variable duration, including some that could not be considered brief psychotherapy because of their length.

Deutsch was a respected member of the psychoanalytic establishment, and he brought this prestige to his new methodology. He always made clear in his writings that what he called "applied psychoanalysis" was different from psychoanalysis proper, and, therefore, he did not face the criticism that he was trying to destroy psychoanalysis, as did some of the previous workers in the field. His interest in "applied psychoanalysis" and sector therapy grew out of and was part of his work with psychosomatically ill patients. During the 1950s there was a general disillusionment with the psychological treatment of psychosomatic illnesses, and perhaps because of the decline in interest in this area, the work of Deutsch had less influence in the subsequent years.

THE CURRENT SITUATION

The current techniques of brief psychotherapy were developed in the late 1950s and early 1960s largely because of the pressure of patients who were waiting to receive long-term analytically oriented psychotherapy and who could not be served by the number of therapists then available. In the United States at that time, psychoanalysis was well established as the theory and treatment of choice at most training centers. Most trainees aspired to be psychoanalysts, and the only desirable training experience prior to, or, if necessary, in lieu of, psychoanalytic training was long-term analytically oriented psychotherapy. In many clinics this was the only treatment offered, with the result that each trainee would treat a small number of patients for a long period of time, while waiting lists became longer and longer as more and more people wanted treatment.

The therapies described in the following chapters were developed (with the exception of Alexander's) around the same time in large urban centers with active training pro-

grams where the primary orientation of the facility was analytic. These therapies were developed independently of one
another, although all were influenced by Alexander. It is probably not a coincidence that these brief therapies were developed at a time when analysis was so firmly established.
Although the mainstream of analytic therapists still regard
brief therapy with considerable skepticism, there is no longer
the type of defensive overreaction evident now that existed
formerly, when any innovation was seen as a threat to analysis. A secure analytic establishment, while perhaps not as
open-minded as it might be, at least has no need for the type
of hostility seen in the past.

The authors whose work is described in the remainder of
this book differ from other writers on brief therapy past and
present in their attempts at offering a complete system of
therapy—that is, the selection of patients, the treatment technique, and the training of therapists are integrated into a
whole that is consistent with the goals being sought. Alexander
was the first to attempt this, but, as noted in the following
chapter, he did not fully succeed in developing a completely
systematic approach. Wolberg is closest to Alexander in creating a continuum between brief and long-term therapy, while
Sifneos, Mann, Malan, and Davanloo all have clear-cut criteria
of selection and technique which distinguish their brief therapies from long-term therapy.

The establishment of specific techniques is of great sig-
nificance. Not only does it permit the replication of these
techniques by others for the purpose of validating the results,
but it permits brief psychotherapy to be established as a
definite subspecialty of psychotherapy. As has been noted,
progress was impeded and much confusion resulted from the
lack of a distinction between psychoanalysis and psychotherapy. While the boundaries are still not firm, there is at this
time some general agreement about the selection criteria,
technique, and training required for psychoanalysis. The new
specific techniques of brief therapy permit brief therapy to be
as clearly delineated from long-term psychotherapy as psychoanalysis is at the other end of the therapeutic spectrum.

3

THE WORK
OF ALEXANDER—
THE EFFICACY OF
BRIEF CONTACT

Alexander serves as the major transition figure between those therapists who developed their own individual attempts at brief psychotherapy and those workers who came after him who developed the systematic approaches that will be discussed in later chapters of this book. In the course of his work Alexander touched on nearly all the aspects of brief psychotherapy that were to be incorporated by the later workers, but he never developed a well-organized system of brief psychotherapy of his own, leaving unanswered the challenge he set in his and French's major work on brief psychotherapy: "to discover in just what cases is such [brief] therapy possible, and to establish the techniques necessary to bring about beneficent results" (Alexander and French 1946, p. 164).

While Alexander began his studies in this area by trying to understand what makes brief psychotherapy work (he was led to this research by the case of a scientist "cured" in two sessions; see Case B below), by the time his and French's book was published in 1946 his focus had shifted from dealing only with brief psychotherapy to an attempt at redefining all aspects of analytically oriented psychotherapy, developing a continuum from the briefest contact to the most extensive classical psychoanalysis. Thus, the book is not entitled *Brief Psychotherapy* but rather *Psychoanalytic Therapy*. By broadening the scope of the work he blurred the distinctions between brief and other forms of psychotherapy.

Alexander's work is based on the treatment of 292 patients through the Chicago Institute for Psychoanalysis and an "almost equal" number of private cases. The patients were treated by Alexander and his colleagues at the Chicago Institute from 1938 through 1945. No formal statistical results of this research were published, although 25 cases are reported in varying detail in his book and elsewhere (Alexander and French 1946, Chicago Institute for Psychoanalysis 1946). There is some information on follow-up, but no formal follow-up studies were done. In the following pages, the material from Alexander is arranged in a manner that should facilitate comparison with current techniques of brief psychotherapy.

AVOIDANCE OF REGRESSION

FREQUENCY OF SESSIONS

Many of Alexander's innovations are designed to avoid regression. While psychoanalysts strived for a complete understanding of all conflicts of the patient, Alexander felt that, while this was useful as a research tool, full analysis and full understanding were usually not necessary to achieve a therapeutic effect. Once it is accepted that a full analysis is not necessary in all cases, it becomes possible to look at the phenomenon of regression, an important tool in psychoanalysis, and determine its optimal usefulness and the means for controlling it.

Alexander emphasizes that there is always a balance in the treatment situation between the pain felt by the patient because of his or her conflicts and the gratification the patient receives from the treatment situation itself. There is a danger in most prolonged treatments that the gratification will become stronger than the pain of the conflict. The gratification occurs especially after there has been some symptom relief, which often happens soon after the start of treatment, and when the negative aspects of the transference such as anger at the therapist and feelings of shame at being dependent on the therapist have been interpreted and alleviated. Once the balance has shifted to the side of gratification, successful treatment will be impossible because there are insufficient forces motivating the patient to conclude the treatment. Alexander believed that the less regression there was in the treatment, the less the possibility of the patient deriving gratification from the treatment.

One of the chief techniques used by Alexander to control the level of regression is changing the frequency of the sessions. According to Alexander, daily sessions are rarely indicated, because with daily sessions the balance of forces between the discomfort and gratification leans toward gratification. Not only is there the gratification of daily contact with the therapist, but also, because of the daily therapy, feelings rarely have the opportunity to build up to uncomfortable levels. For most therapy, Alexander recommends once-a-week sessions, although at the beginning of treatment, in order to hasten the development of the transference, more frequent sessions are often useful. He also recommends more frequent sessions at times of particular stress, whether external or caused by the treatment, for example, when particularly painful material is emerging or at times of severe resistance. Interruption of the treatment is a useful tool in controlling the development of regression and dependency. Alexander uses interruptions in order to make the patient aware of his or her dependency feelings. He feels that as long as the patient's dependency feelings are being gratified, he or she will not become aware of them and therefore will not be able to bring them into the treatment. (This is similar to the well-known experience that much material is elicited by the therapist's vacation, although with Alexander it is under the control of the therapist rather than under the control of the calendar.) Interruptions are also used prior to termination to allow the patient to try out what has been learned and convince himself or herself that he or she is ready to terminate. Interruptions in therapy lasting from 1 to 18 months have been used by Alexander in this way.

It will be apparent that Alexander rarely uses the couch and that most of the treatment is done sitting up, face-to-face.

INTERPRETATIONS

Everything need not be interpreted. Alexander (1956) stresses the distinction between regression as a defense and regression to the level of the basic conflict. If the regression is defensive, that is, regression from an oedipal conflict in order to experience the safety of an earlier stage of development, it need not be interpreted but can be ignored. Obviously much time can be saved by not interpreting all the material, while at the same time not reinforcing and gratifying the patient for his or her regressive productions. Alexander believes that not all neurotic symptoms stem from early childhood conflicts, but that some are the result of later traumata. If such is the case, it is not necessary to deal with periods *before* the development of the conflict. The therapist should look for the period of time when the patient refused "to grow up" and then avoid material from earlier periods.

Regression can also be avoided by making *early* transference interpretations (Chicago Institute for Psychoanalysis 1946). This will make the patient more aware of the phenomenon of transference and will make it less likely for a regressive transference to develop. With the adult, observing ego keeping a watch on the treatment, it is much harder for the patient to allow a childlike dependency to flourish.

ACTIVITY OF THERAPIST AND PATIENT

Alexander stresses activity. Treatment should result from active planning on the part of the therapist. The therapist should maintain a high level of activity throughout the treatment. He or she is not limited to listening to the free associations of the patient but can direct the questions or otherwise control the material. The therapist can offer direct suggestions to the patient in order to influence his or her daily life if the therapist feels it will help the treatment. Pressure is required to keep the patient from dwelling unnecessarily on the past and thus avoiding his or her present problem. The therapist continually encourages the patient to apply what is learned in therapy to the current life situation.

At the same time the *patient* is urged to be active in the treatment. It is made clear that the patient has responsibility in making the treatment a success. He or she is urged to participate during the sessions and to work on the material between sessions. Intellectual understanding is not sufficient; it is necessary for the patient to apply this understanding in real life situations while the treatment is still going on.

THE CORRECTIVE EMOTIONAL EXPERIENCE AND THE USE OF THE TRANSFERENCE

Much controversy has surrounded Alexander's concept of the corrective emotional experience. Alexander believed that the patient should reexperience the original conflict during the course of therapy. If the original conflict were reexperienced, and the patient could observe it with his or her adult capabilities, it would seem less frightening than it seemed in the unconscious. If the patient received a response that was more benign than what had been experienced originally, or feared that he or she would experience, while a child, this would provide an excellent learning experience for the patient, proving that now things could be different. Put in this way, the concept hardly seems controversial. It became controversial because Alexander stated that this is what "cures," that the corrective emotional experience is *necessary* before there can be any therapeutic effect of treatment and that insight and the recovery of childhood memories *follows* the corrective emotional experience. That is, once the ego has been strengthened by the corrective emotional experience it will be able to withstand the childhood memories and affects and they will then emerge. It is apparent that it is not necessary to resolve this controversy in order to agree that it is useful in any analytically oriented treatment for the childhood conflict to be reexperienced, as fully as possible, in the therapeutic situation, with the therapist providing a different response from that provided by the original parent figure.

Alexander emphasized that the corrective emotional experience can occur in the treatment situation, but it can also occur in relation to other important figures in the patient's actual life. The implications of this are great, for it means that transference to the therapist need not necessarily become the central aspect of the treatment. If the circumstances are conducive to it, the entire conflict can be relived and worked through in relation to someone outside the therapy. In such a situation there will be relatively few transference interpretations (see Case P below).

In most treatments, however, the transference to the therapist will serve as the vehicle for the corrective emotional experience. For these situations Alexander advocates "manipulation" of the transference. By this he means trying to determine, on the basis of a full psychodynamic history, what type of "personality" in the therapist will most likely provide the corrective emotional experience for the patient. Thus, if a woman's father was harsh and demanding, the therapist will try to appear benign and accepting. If the father was passive and overly permissive, the therapist will set limits where he or she can. This aspect of Alexander's technique has received perhaps the least acceptance. Most therapists dislike the idea of manipulation, even in the service of helping the patient. Also, most therapists probably do not have the acting skills necessary to carry off a consistent and sincere performance of the predesigned transference model.

THE FOCUS

Alexander pays little direct attention to the concept of the focus, though by implication he is much aware of it. By minimizing regression and restricting the therapy to the level of the most recent conflict, the therapist keeps the therapy on a focus. Indeed, Alexander provides a theoretical basis for the success of brief therapies where the focus is not necessarily the nuclear conflict. He believed that the resolution of a limited conflict will lead to the growth that was impeded by that conflict. This growth in turn increases self-esteem as a result of the patient's feelings of success and accomplishment. The patient will then be in a better position to work alone to improve other areas of his or her life. "Every success encourages new trials and decreases inferiority feelings, resentments, and their sequelae" (Alexander and French 1946, p. 40). (Here Alexander anticipates Caplan's theory of crisis resolution [1964] where mastery of one crisis leads to growth in the capacity of the individual to master future crises.) Thus, by not requiring that all conflicts be solved, but by trying to solve the most important and letting the patient work on the others independently, a focus is maintained.

Alexander's manipulation of the transference also results in focality, as those elements of the patient's productions that refer to aspects of the therapist that are different from the role which the therapist is trying to assume will tend to be ignored.

Thus, while a focus is not agreed upon by the patient and therapist, the therapist makes a formulation of the central conflict for himself or herself at the beginning of the treatment, and then, unless the evidence forces a change, the therapist tries to work within that formulation.

TIME LIMIT

Alexander does not set a definite time limit. He does not state whether he or his group ever worked with a fixed time limit, but mentions that Ferenczi and Rank tried it and gave it up. He does, however, clearly and repeatedly indicate to the patient that the therapy will not be a prolonged one. The idea that there is as much time as is wanted leads to procrastination and the development of regression and gratification from the process of the therapy. The therapies reported by Alexander range from 2 to 65 sessions over a period of 17 months. Alexander does not pay special attention to issues of termination.

How long a treatment will last depends on the "degree of intensity the patient's ego can endure in the transference experience without resorting to regressive evasion" (Alexander and French 1946, p. 163). If the conflict is worked through in relation to someone outside the therapeutic situation, the same criterion applies. Thus, the stronger the patient's ego, the harder the therapist can press the patient, and the shorter the therapy will be.

TECHNIQUES

Alexander states that there are no basic differences in technique between brief and long-term therapy. (When the modifications of technique which have already been noted are considered, and when Alexander states that there is a continuum between these therapies and psychoanalysis, it is understandable that psychoanalysts have been critical of him.) A complete history is taken early in the treatment so that the therapist can make a psychodynamic formulation and an assessment of the patient's strengths and weaknesses. The patient is observed in order to determine his or her characteristic mode of reacting to the therapist. Trial interpretations are used to gauge psychological mindedness and the tenacity of the patient's resistances. On the basis of all this information a treatment plan is made. This plan will include an indication of the approximate length of treatment, the optimum transference role for the therapist, the level of the conflict that will be focused on, and an assessment of how vigorously the resistances of the patient can be confronted.

Once the treatment commences Alexander uses the full range of psychotherapeutic techniques, in addition to those special techniques that have been discussed earlier. Thus he will analyze resistances and defenses, allow the patient periods of free association, and work with slips, fantasies, and dreams. He found that in the briefer therapies dreams tend to reflect more what is happening in the treatment and in everyday life and have less connection to events in the past.

Interpretations are made on as deep a level as the material warrants. Early conflicts are reexperienced both intellectually and affectually. Transference is interpreted as well as experienced. Alexander belongs to the radical school of brief psychotherapy, demonstrating that long-term change can occur as a result of a deep interpretive approach.

SELECTION OF PATIENTS

Alexander is weak on defining selection criteria. He states his techniques are suitable for mild chronic and acute neurosis as well as "incipient" emotional problems, which are not clearly defined. He finds no correlation between the severity of the symptoms and the length of the treatment needed in order to obtain good results. He believes psychoanalysis (which he refers to as the "standard technique") should be reserved for severe chronic neurosis. Other factors mentioned in selection are ego-strength (not further defined) and good motivation. Trial interpretations are used and are a good indicator of how a patient will do in treatment. Eisenstein (1980) states that in his practice Alexander used the patient's psychological mindedness and capacity for insight as selection criteria.

COUNTERTRANSFERENCE PROBLEMS

The chief countertransference problem that arises using Alexander's techniques occurs with the manipulation of the transference by assuming a predetermined transference role. If the therapist either does not fully believe in the concept, or is poor in the execution of the assumed transference role, the therapy will lose its authenticity and therefore will not be successful. Because apparently few workers have adopted this technique, there is little data on how this manipulation of the transference works in hands other than Alexander's. Other problems of this technique come from the use of techniques common to long forms of psychotherapy. Unless the therapist is constantly vigilant it is easy for the brief therapy to drift into a long-term therapy, because there are no distinctive technical factors or time limits to remind the therapist of the intended brevity of the treatment.

RESULTS

According to Alexander, the results obtained are comparable to those of long-term psychotherapy. There is not only symptom removal but characerological change, and "profound changes in the dynamic structure of the personality" are seen (Chicago Institute for Psychoanalysis 1946, p. 37). While individual case reports are given, there are no statistics on results available. There are no published verbatim transcripts of treatments; so one cannot get an exact picture of what Alexander actually did in the course of his therapy.

CASE MATERIAL

Alexander never oganized his material in a fully systematic way. Much of his and French's book consists of case reports by therapists in Alexander's group. The material shows that a wide variety of clinical conditions were treated, using rather divergent techniques. It is impossible to understand fully what Alexander was trying to do without studying the case material.

For this reason, illustrative case summaries are given in some detail. The cases are labeled with the letters used by Alexander in the book.

Case A

This case illustrates the usefulness of manipulating the transference.

A successful 42-year-old manufacturer came to see Alexander because of a long history of irritability and difficulty in getting along with people, uncontrollable jerking movements of his arms of several years' duration, and a complete loss of potency in the preceding few months. Significant in the past history was a father who dominated everyone in the family and in his business and who belittled the patient throughout his childhood. The patient's mother died when he was 10 years old. The father died when the patient was 30, and the patient took over the father's business, running it successfully, but he adopted the same dominating attitudes toward his wife and son that his father had adopted toward the patient and his mother. The patient's wife divorced him, but remarried him a year and a half later without any improvement in the domestic relationship. There were no noted precipitants to the impotence.

The treatment consisted of 26 interviews and lasted ten weeks. Within the first two interviews the patient attempted to recreate his old relationship with his father within the therapeutic situation. On the one hand, he strictly followed all advice that the therapist gave him; on the other hand, he was extremely competitive with the therapist. He responded to interpretations by telling the therapist stories of how successful he was in business. Alexander felt that had he remained the traditional, neutral therapist, the patient would have continued his old patterns with the therapist. He would have seen the therapist as authoritarian and judgmental, and this would have justified his rebellion against the therapist without inducing any guilt in himself. There would have been no progress in the treatment. Instead, Alexander tried in every way to be different from the father. He was not arbitrary and he allowed the patient to determine the frequency of the sessions, to determine whether he used the couch or chair, and he did not comment when the patient walked around the room during the sessions. He was supportive of the work the patient did and deprecated his own knowledge and the knowledge of psychiatrists in general. When the patient remained competitive despite this attitude on the part of the therapist, the therapist was able to show the patient that his competitiveness came from within himself. This led to the mobilization of guilt in the patient and to an improvement in his behavior toward his wife and son.

During the 18th session the patient reported a dream in which the therapist smashed glassware that the patient had manufactured. The patient recalled in association that his father had once smashed a set of glassware in a rage. During this session, Alexander, again acting in a manner opposite to that of the father, asked in an interested manner about the patient's work. The patient gave a long, didactic, and condescending talk to the therapist. This session was followed by the return of the patient's potency. Alexander feels the potency returned because the patient's self-confidence increased as a result of his being able to assume authority over the therapist. The tolerant and encouraging atmosphere of the treatment also allowed the patient gradually to emancipate himself from the father's intimidation.

After a further series of dreams showing confusion as to whether the father or the therapist was helpful or dominating, the therapist was able to show the patient that he was unable to accept help from the therapist, or from anyone else, without feeling inferior and unmanly. His excessive competitiveness was interpreted as a reaction to the wish for, and the fear of, getting help. During these sessions the patient maintained his improved attitude toward his wife and son. His uncontrolled movements had disappeared and his potency continued unimpaired. Treatment was discontinued for two months and the improvement was maintained at the next session. The treatment was then stopped. There is a nine-month follow-up report, where the symptomatic and characterological changes had continued.

Case B

This is Alexander's first brief therapy case, successfully treated in two sessions.

A prominent 51-year-old scientist came to see Alexander in a state of "extreme agitation" complaining of feelings of exhaustion, inability to sleep, and inability to talk without crying. While he had had three similar episodes during the preceding three years, the current episode, of six weeks duration, was by far the worst. The patient had been working hard on a scientific project during the past three years, and the results were due to be presented at a national convention a few weeks after the initial interview. He had been trying to complete his work, and, while he had made substantial progress, he could not completely solve the last problem he was working on. He had developed an antipathy to his work, had decided not to present it at the convention, and wanted to give the paper to his collaborators to read, insisting that his name not appear on it.

The history, obtained in the course of the two interviews, revealed that the patient was the only child of parents who had married each other late in life, each having had six children by previous marriages. He said he was spoiled by his parents. As a child he had a mild case of poliomyelitis and was thereafter treated as weaker and more vulnerable than the other children. His only outstanding attribute was his mathematical ability which he used in order to excel and on one occasion used to embarrass a teacher in high school. His first marriage was unhappy, the patient having premature ejaculations, the wife drinking and being unfaithful to the patient. After three years the marriage ended and subsequently the patient had a happy and enduring second marriage. However, three years before coming to treatment, the patient began to note a decrease in his sexual functioning.

During the first interview Alexander was impressed with the patient's emphasis on his altruism in his work, that he worked not for fame but for "human welfare." The therapist pointed out to the patient in the first interview that he was denying his "selfishness," that is, the gratification that he would receive from solving a difficult problem. Alexander tempered the interpretation by pointing out that the patient was indeed also unselfish, but that all behavior is overdetermined and that all people have some selfishness. The patient experienced relief of symptoms after the first interview. He returned for the second interview saying that he was impressed with the therapist's ability to explain his problems in an organized and "rational" manner. He had never thought of himself as having unconscious feelings and attitudes, but was now willing to entertain this concept. He realized as a result of his first interview that he was indeed a very competitive person. He felt he could accept this about himself because the therapist had assured him that all people were competitive.

During the second interview the therapist pointed out the temporal connection between the patient's declining sexual potency and his increased emphasis on his work. The patient picked up on this, asking if the work was a "compensation" for his declining potency. This led to a discussion of the patient's feeling that, if he did not complete his work, no one else would be able to do it. He then "with a sudden flash of insight" confessed that he began the current work in order to disprove a widely held scientific concept. At this point in the treatment the patient was able to acknowledge his competitiveness and assertiveness, but when the therapist told him that he was also afraid of the competition of the younger generation, he could not accept this. By showing the patient how he had competed with his older brothers and his teachers, he was able to get the patient to accept the idea that he had once wanted to vanquish the older generation and that his work was the means by which he vanquished them. Because his work was his weapon for vanquishing rivals, he also had feelings of guilt about succeeding with his work. His withdrawal from the project at the last minute was a way of attacking his younger collaborators:

. . . as if to say, "Well go ahead, you young giants. Do it without me, if you can. But you cannot. You need me!" The analyst continued in a dramatic fashion. "And they come and beg you. But you remain adamant. You say, 'No, I am going to retire; I have had enough of fight and struggle. You do it yourself!' You are taking a malicious satisfaction in their impotence to solve the mathematical equations. In your own eyes you are fully rehabilitated. You can say, 'I may no longer be a great hero in the field of sexuality, but I am still better than the younger generation. I am better in what really counts.' All this you cannot permit yourself to feel frankly. You must have some alibi, and this you receive from your illness. You are depressed, you cannot sleep, you cannot stop weeping, you do not want any recognition. Why should you feel guilty? In this way you can have satisfaction and still not feel bad about it because at the same time that you hurt others you also hurt yourself. But would you be so generous if you were not sure they could not accomplish your work without you? sure that even if they could, they would certainly give you the credit? Your martyrdom is only a cover for a vindictive triumph over your colleagues —whose only crime is that they are younger than you. (Alexander and French 1946, p. 151)

The patient responded to this by saying that this was the first time in his life that he could speak freely about himself, that he now felt quite differently about himself and his work, and that he would consult the therapist again if he needed him. A few months later the patient informed Alexander that he had completed his work and presented his paper at the convention. A follow-up of eight years revealed that the patient had had a few mild depressive episodes but no return of the major symptoms which brought him to treatment. He was still actively at work at the time of the follow-up interview.

This treatment was completed in two sessions. The main reason for the success of the treatment was Alexander's intuitive feeling that he could make relatively deep interpretations in a few sessions. In retrospect, some of the factors enabling this therapy to succeed can be understood. The patient came to treatment with high expectations deriving in part from Alexander's prominent position in his community. One can speculate that some of the grandeur that the patient wanted for himself was displaced onto Alexander. Clearly the patient was motivated to try to understand himself. He not only worked during the sessions, but also between the first and second meeting. He responded well to a partial interpretation (the connection between his failing potency and his work). The intellectual framework in insight-oriented psychotherapy was consonant with his own orientation as a scientist, but Alexander did not allow the therapy to be merely intellectual. By using his dramatic formulations he made the treatment an affectually meaningful one as well (here Alexander anticipates Sifneos's often dramatic interventions). As was noted above, it was the treatment of this patient that led Alexander to study the phenomenon of brief therapy.

Case I*

In this treatment, the patient receives relief for her acute symptoms, and long-standing characterological patterns are changed.

A 32-year-old woman came for treatment because of feelings of severe depression concerning her pregnancy, then in its seventh month. Pregnancy made her feel inferior and dirty. She also complained of feelings of depression and inadequacy throughout her life. Since the birth of her only child, seven years previously, she had had feelings of disappointment, regrets at not having a career, and feelings of doubt as to her adequacy as a mother. The treatment plan was to see the patient weekly until after the birth and then to have more intensive therapy, but the treatment was progressing so well that the once-weekly sessions were continued for a total of 42 sessions.

The patient was the second of seven children. The father was a teacher of philosophy in a series of small denominational colleges. His attitude in the home reflected the rigidity and strict morality of his religious denomination. The mother was intellectually ambitious for herself and her children, and the patient felt that her wish to have a career stemmed in part from the wish not to disappoint her mother. Her next youngest sister was

* This patient was treated by Catherine L. Bacon.

the father's favorite, and the patient always put this sister's needs ahead of her own. She stayed home after finishing high school to help care for the younger children, and when it was time for her sister to go to college the patient went to work to help her sister. Only upon her sister's urging did she turn to her own education.

Initially the therapy focused on the patient's attitudes toward her pregnancy. During the first interview the therapist told the patient that her attitudes were probably related to her feeling that her mother had done something wrong in becoming pregnant. This led to a discussion of the repressive attitude toward sexuality in the home, the patient's ignorance of sexual matters, and memories linking childbirth with violence. The feelings about the pregnancy were dealt with during the seven sessions preceding the birth. In addition to the idea that having a child indicated that a person was sexual and therefore bad, the other theme to emerge during this time was the feeling that the patient would be an inadequate parent. Only her mother and favored sister should have children.

After the birth of the child, a daughter, the patient's competitiveness with her sister began to be discussed. The patient's defense against her competitiveness was to present herself as hopelessly inadequate, and she frequently told the therapist how hopeless a treatment case she was. A typical episode from this phase of the treatment occurred when a male member of her club told her he thought she was "quite a person." She replied, "No, I'm only the wife of a successful man." Following this compliment she made a great effort to get a friend, who reminded her of her sister, elected as president of the club. Through the analysis of incidents like this, as well as through the analysis of dreams and fantasies, it became clear that the patient believed that any success, social or intellectual, would lead to the husbands of her friends becoming fascinated with her and leaving their wives for her. It was possible to connect this fantasy with her wish to excel and take her sister's and mother's place with her father. Her depression, inactivity, and feelings of inadequacy were seen as a defense against this wish. Her feelings of guilt at wanting things for herself were reinforced by the family's attitude that taking anything for oneself, especially if it was pleasurable, was wrong. These conflicts were not only interpreted by the therapist, but the therapist also actively encouraged the patient to enjoy herself and to participate in more social and intellectual activities. By the time the therapy was concluded, the patient was feeling much better about herself as a person and as a mother. She dreamt that she was a social success with her brother-in-law after she allowed him to see how intelligent she was. The dream was a pleasurable one, without feelings of guilt. Follow-up was only of a "few months." In that interval, the patient had moved to a different city. She reported that she was feeling well and was able to enjoy her relationship with her husband and children much better than previously. She no longer felt inadequate, nor did she feel that she need not enjoy life.

This patient would probably have been taken into "standard" analytic treatment had not external circumstances mitigated against it at the beginning. The therapist was alert and open-minded enough to continue with once-weekly treatment even when more frequent sessions became feasible, because the treatment was progressing so well at that point. What factors contributed to this success? The patient was highly motivated and worked well, not only in the sessions but between the sessions as well. She was psychologically minded and readily produced much meaningful material including memories, fantasies, and dreams. The patient's characterological passivity and feelings of inadequacy were seen to be a defense against oedipal striving, so that when this conflict was worked with, extensive characterological changes in the patient became possible. The authors emphasize favorable conditions in the patient's actual life situation. She had a good marriage. She really wanted to be a good mother, and when the defenses against this were analyzed, it freed her to enjoy her actual role. In this therapy there was little overt attention paid to transference material. The main conflict was made vivid through the patient's feelings about her children, the birth during the course of therapy being a particular focus of much of the material. The therapist did provide active encouragement, giving permission for the patient's enjoyment and growth, whereas the actual parents had been prohibitive and critical in similar situations during the patient's childhood.

Case P*

This unusual case illustrates the high degree of focality with an intense abreaction within the transference.

A very intelligent 19-year-old came for treatment because of feelings of depression severe enough to interfere with his studies at a technical school. He was due to enter the army three months hence and external circumstances limited each session to 20 minutes. There was a total of 35 sessions during the three months of the therapy.

The patient's mother died in a fire when he was three years old, and until he was eight the patient thought that his stepmother was his real mother. When the stepmother told him of his mother, he stated that he "felt stunned" but made no comment at the time. He had ambivalent feelings toward his father, who, though now a skilled laborer, had been for many years the successful owner of a series of gambling houses. He admired his father's skills as a gambler but was ashamed of his previous occupation, telling his friends that his father was an electrical engineer.

During the first interview the therapist noted the patient's reluctance to speak of his mother's death. She asked how he got along with women. He replied, "You seem to be receding further and further into the distance." This early transference response proved to be a forerunner of a rapid intense transference that was dealt with openly throughout by the therapist. Early in the treatment it became evident that the stepmother was openly seductive with the patient. He became increasingly tense and resentful in the treatment situation, and the therapist pointed out his fears of seduction by her. He denied this and left treatment for a week, returned, and asked to lie on the couch so he would not have to see her; but after a few sessions he went back to sitting in a chair.

The patient's schoolwork began to improve. He spoke of feeling that everyone had always seemed cold to him. He said that all his life he had been "looking for something in reality that is familiar, that I knew a long time ago. I

* This patient was treated by Adelaide McFadyen Johnson.

don't know what it can be. It is something steadying. Some day I feel I'll find it." The therapist related this to the death of the mother, but the patient avoided the issue. The therapist decided to focus the rest of the treatment on the loss of the mother and all subsequent interpretations were directed toward this focus.

After two months the patient seemed ready to deal with the issue. He reported that he had obtained the mother's birth certificate to learn her maiden name, which he had never known. When asked what the name was, he had forgotten it. He then reported telling his father a dream in which the patient had set the fire which killed the mother. This led to interpretations of his having been angry at the mother. He replied by indicating that he must have been bad, because no relative would take him in after the mother's death. The therapist then asked him for his mother's name. He handed over all the papers in the wallet while looking for the birth certificate, but when he found it, he gave the name and then put the certificate away. The therapist pointed out that he wanted to hold onto the mother for himself, indicating love as well as anger. The patient, with a faraway look in his eye, said he wanted to get a picture of his mother. He then began sobbing, threw himself on the couch, and cried for ten minutes. He then said, with great feeling, "Silly, but I feel as if my own mother were all around me here. It's something so familiar." Obviously moved, the patient then asked the therapist for all sorts of advice concerning sex, religion, etcetera. "Talk to me as you would to an adolescent." At the end of the interview the patient said that he had been talking to his mother and that he felt wonderful. (The patient was speaking metaphorically. He did not develop a transference psychosis.) For the remaining two weeks of the therapy the patient applied himself to his schoolwork with enthusiasm. He was no longer depressed. He could see and deal with his parents more realistically. After he entered the army, the patient wrote to the therapist occasionally and visited her "socially" on two occasions. A two-year follow-up report showed that he was feeling and functioning well and that he had a better relationship with people than ever before in his life. The author notes that the real test of the treatment will be in his heterosexual relationships, and no information was available on that issue at the time the material was written.

This treatment, in contrast to the previous case (I), was carried out almost entirely through the transference. The patient produced transference material in the first session, and the therapist picked up on it. Once the focus was decided on, the therapist stayed within it for the rest of the treatment. It is to be noted that the abreaction came after the angry feelings toward the mother had surfaced. That is, the abreaction was possible only after interpretation and was not merely a response to a kindly and giving woman. However, it is doubtful if such a strong reaction would have been possible with a male therapist.

SUMMARY

Alexander's is a radical technique, seeking extensive symptom relief and characterological changes using the usual techniques of psychotherapy. There is emphasis on limiting regression by flexible spacing of sessions, early interpretation of transference, avoiding most regressive material, and encouraging modification of the patient's behavior in the current life situation. The focus of the therapy is the point at which the patient "stopped growing," that is, the latest developmental phase or age at which a significant conflict can be found. Alexander believes that successful therapy occurs as a result of the "corrective emotional experience," which is a repetition in the transference, or with another person in the current life situation, of the central conflict, this time the patient experiencing the conflict in a more benign way. In order to facilitate the corrective emotional experience the therapist should "manipulate" the transference by behaving in such a way as to maximize the possibility of the corrective emotional experience occurring. Selection criteria are not clearly defined, but such factors as ego-strength, motivation, response to trial interpretation, and psychological mindedness are used to evaluate patients. No set time limits are used, and therapies reported range from 1 to 65 sessions. There has been no formal follow-up study.

4

THE SHORT-TERM ANXIETY-PROVOKING PSYCHOTHERAPY OF SIFNEOS

THE MAN WHO WANTED TO GET MARRIED

In August 1956 a 28-year-old man came to the Massachusetts General Hospital for help in overcoming the severe anxiety which was interfering with his plans to be married in November of that year. In addition to the anxiety, he had a number of phobias and multiple somatic complaints. While the present intensity of the symptoms was of recent onset, dating from his decision to get married two months previously, he had a history of phobias in childhood. The phobias began recurring two years earlier after an episode of fainting while in the army.

The patient was not accepted by the regular psychiatric clinic at the hospital. His goal of obtaining symptom relief prior to his marriage was not viewed as being realistically attainable. One evaluator felt that three years of psychotherapy would be required. The patient came to the attention of Peter Sifneos because of other research that Sifneos was doing at that time. Although he had had little experience with short-term therapy, Dr. Sifneos decided to try to help the patient in the seven weeks then remaining before the wedding and proceeded with weekly psychotherapy. What ensued was a dynamically rich therapy lasting six sessions. It was characterized by the patient's high motivation to understand himself, which yielded much dynamically meaningful material. The therapist actively encouraged the patient's efforts. In addition, he made transference interpretations early in the treatment. During the course of this short therapy it was possible for the patient and therapist to understand the current symptoms in relation to the patient's sexual explorations at age four, his father's death shortly thereafter, sexual wishes for his mother, and death wishes for his stepfather at age eight, the latter associated with castration anxieties. The treatment did not merely lead to intellectual insights but was laden with intense affect. As a result of the therapy, the patient's anxieties diminished, and he was able to proceed with the wedding. A three-and-a-half-year follow-up confirmed that the improvements were lasting.

Sifneos was impressed with this remarkable treatment and its results. Like many other creative scientists, he did not merely remark on this unusual phenomenon but rather decided to study the treatment of this patient in order to learn what the essential elements of the brief therapy were. Thus, Sifneos began his research into brief psychotherapy. At first he accepted only quite healthy, well-motivated patients in crisis, but he found that this provided too few cases to work with. Since 1960 he has further developed and used the selection criteria and techniques which will be described in detail in the following pages. The main elements derive from the treatment of the first patient: careful selection, an active confronting technique with early transference interpretation, working with oedipal material directly, and rapid termination with relatively little working through of the separation process.

SELECTION OF PATIENTS

THE FORMAL CRITERIA

As will be seen, careful selection is absolutely essential for Sifneos's therapy, and he has spent considerable time formulating and defining strict selection criteria, which he now states as follows (Sifneos 1972).

The ability of the patient to have a circumscribed chief complaint. This criterion is one of the quickest ways to separate patients who will do well with this short-term therapy from those who will require longer care. A patient who is too vague to be able to focus on one issue will not do well. If there are multiple, seemingly unconnected problems which the patient feels must be solved, there is obviously not enough time in this method of treatment to accomplish these goals. Even more important as a selection criterion is the patient's ability to select one complaint from a number of complaints and to decide to work on that and that alone. The ability to do this indicates a willingness to accept a certain amount of frustration and the realistic limitations which are necessary for this treatment. Furthermore, for this treatment it is necessary that the patient have sufficient ego-strength to work within an oedipal focus without becoming involved in preoedipal or characterological issues (see *The Oedipal Focus* below). The ability to isolate one symptom or conflict area from the rest is a good indicator of this ego-strength. (Obviously, delusions or fixed hypochondriacal symptoms, though circumscribed, do not lend themselves to this treatment.)

Evidence of give and take or meaningful relationship with another person during childhood. This is perhaps the least carefully defined of Sifneos's selection criteria. What he is looking for here is the ability to develop mature object relations, and this, of course, is also hard to define. The emphasis is on "give and take" and altruism as seen with at least one significant figure from the past. It is measured by the ability to recall and give examples of such a relationship during the initial evaluation. It is felt that without such a history the patient will not be able to experience the give and take with the therapist that is needed for the treatment to proceed satisfactorily. (Give and take as used by Sifneos refers to an active reciprocal relationship with a significant other, in contrast to the type of relationship seen in people with character disorders, that is, passive, narcissistic, schizoid, etcetera.) Other measures of "meaningful" include evidence of feelings of intimacy, trust, and real emotional involvement. It can be seen that borderline patients will not be able to fulfill this criterion.

Capacity to relate flexibly to the evaluator during the interview and to experience and express feelings freely. Flexibility, as used here, means not only the ability to react appropriately to a wide variety of topics and to changes of attitude on the part of the interviewer, but also means the ability to get some distance from the matter at hand, to evaluate it realistically, and to see other points of view, while not necessarily agreeing with everything that the evaluator says. (In this sense, flexible is the opposite of dogmatic.) Particular attention is paid to the range and appropriateness of affect throughout the evaluation interview. Again, it is not only the expression of affect that is important, but also some ability to step back and to recognize and realistically evaluate the affect that has been expressed, adding a cognitive component to the affective expression.

Above-average intelligence and psychological sophistication. The intelligence is not measured by I.Q. tests but is derived from the history of high achievement in school or work situations. A good estimate of intelligence can also often be made from the patient's responses during the evaluation interview. Psychological sophistication means the ability to see phenomena in psychological terms rather than the ability to use psychological jargon. A naive patient who is willing to look at himself or herself honestly and recognize that symptoms may be related to intrapsychic processes would be accepted, while a well-educated person who knows all the right words but deep down *really* believes his or her stomach pains are due to an undiagnosed physical illness, despite all negative medical tests, would be rejected for this treatment.

Intelligence is an important requirement for this treatment because much of its effectiveness comes from the patient's ability to grasp intellectual formulations of past problems and then utilize these formulations in order to solve current and eventually future conflict situations. Intelligence is also needed to grasp the therapist's frequent attempts to tie material from the past and current situations together, often in fairly complex ways. As will be seen, the patient's cognitive awareness is used not only for problem solving, but is also used by the patient to help control the intense affect which is often mobilized during the course of treatment. A readiness to work psychologically is necessary because the structure and time frame of the treatment do not permit education of the patient in these matters, nor can resistances to looking at oneself be worked through adequately in this brief therapy.

Motivation for change and not for symptom relief. This criterion is so important that it is divided into seven subcategories by which motivation is measured. Meeting six or seven of the categories is considered good motivation; five is considered fair motivation; four, questionable motivation; and less than four, unmotivated.

An ability to recognize that the symptoms are psychological. Here one considers not only the general psychological awareness and sophistication of the patient, as indicated above, but whether the specific symptoms which are to be worked on by the patient are recognized as being amenable to psychological treatment.

A tendency to be introspective and give an honest and truthful account of emotional difficulties. Introspection is required to help move the treatment along and to eliminate those whose primary defenses are projection and acting out. This criterion also eliminates those patients who use rationalization and intellectualization as a major defense. If these patients are accepted, the treatment could easily turn into a meaningless intellectual exercise or into a fruitless series of arguments with the therapist.

Willingness to participate actively in the treatment situation. This important criterion eliminates patients who will respond passively to the interventions of the therapist. Because the therapist is so active and confronting in his technique, it is important that the patient be able to hold his or her own lest the therapy turn into a one-sided event wherein the therapist meaninglessly belabors the patient with the confrontations and interpretations. A good patient for anxiety-provoking short-term therapy is one who fights back during the evaluation interview, indicating that he or she will be an active participant in the treatment.

Curiosity and willingness to understand oneself. An active, goal-directed curiosity obviously enhances therapy.

Realistic expectations of the results of psychotherapy. This is a corollary of the ability to pick a circumscribed focus and indicates an ability for good reality testing and the ability to accept realistic limitations and frustrations.

Willingness to make reasonable sacrifices. This refers to

putting oneself out for the treatment if necessary, for example, in regard to fees and to time commitments. How much one is willing to give up for a treatment is obviously a good measure of motivation, although no attempt is made to create artificial barriers if none actually exist.

THE EVALUATION INTERVIEW

During the initial interview, the therapist needs to collect enough data to obtain: "1) the complete biographical history taking and reformulation of the presenting complaints; 2) the specific criteria for selection; 3) the psychodynamic formulation, therapeutic focus, and contract; 4) the specification of criteria for successful outcome" (Sifneos 1979, p. 13). Sifneos believes that this information can be gathered in one 45 to 60 minute session, even by a relatively unskilled therapist (Davanloo 1978). It is apparent from this that the initial evaluation must be a very active process, and, indeed, it would seem that the activity itself becomes part of the selection process. That is, the patient's response to the evaluation technique will show itself in both intellectual and affectual reactions, which in turn will determine the individual's suitability for the treatment. A patient who is displeased by the interviewer and reacts with passivity, sullenness, withdrawal, and inhibition of material will not meet the selection criteria. On the other hand, a patient who responds actively and positively will be more likely to be accepted. Thus the very active evaluation becomes a screening technique for those who will do well in this very active therapy (see also, Golden 1978).

The history taking should be a complete one, as it is necessary to obtain enough data to make a psychodynamic formulation as well as to be sure that serious psychopathology is not overlooked. Because, as will be seen, attention will be paid to the oedipal conflict, special note is made of the patient's relationship with parents and siblings in early childhood and again at puberty. Adult relationships are also evaluated carefully. Sifneos finds it useful to ask for the patient's earliest memory or the earliest event in his or her life about which he or she has been told. If the material warrants it, trial interpretations may be made during the evaluation interview. The patient's response to the interpretation will provide valuable information about his or her psychological mindedness and ability to utilize psychodynamic psychotherapy. In addition, the patient's response may provide corroboration of the psychodynamic formulation which underlay the interpretation.

At the end of the evaluation, if the patient is found acceptable for short-term anxiety-provoking psychotherapy, he or she is asked to agree to work on one specific symptom or area of conflict. The therapist, on his or her own, has made a psychodynamic formulation, tying the symptoms of the current conflict together with events from the past, but it is not presented to the patient at this time unless the patient has already made the connections as a result of the interview. The area to be worked on is presented to the patient in derivative terms, often in the form of a question. For example, based on the data, a male patient may be asked whether he feels it is more important to work on his difficulties in getting close to women or on his difficulties relating to men in authority. If the patient cannot readily decide on one issue, the therapist works with the patient until one is selected, preferably the one the therapist thinks is the most meaningful. If the therapist has evidence that one issue is more important than the one the patient selects, he or she can present this evidence to the patient in order to try to influence the patient's choice. The patient is then told that the therapy will be brief, lasting "several months." It will be noted that *no* definite time limit is set at the beginning of this treatment. (If the evaluation is done by someone other than the therapist who will be treating the patient, the treating therapist takes his or her own history and comes to a decision with the patient as to which issue will be worked on.)

If the therapist is not sure at the end of the first evaluation interview as to the suitability of the patient for this treatment, another evaluation interview may be done, often by a therapist of the opposite sex. This has proven to be helpful, as patterns of behavior at times emerge more clearly as a result.

THE OEDIPAL FOCUS

Only patients whose core conflict is thought to be at an oedipal level are accepted for this form of therapy. That is, the origins of the conflicts leading to the current symptoms or difficulties are seen to be the result of an earlier triangular situation rather than the result of preoedipal or dyadic conflict. Sifneos feels that these latter situations are not amenable to this form of treatment. Among those patients with oedipal conflicts, Sifneos has found the best results occur when the basic relationship with the parent of the opposite sex was a positive one and when the current symptoms are due to a real but relatively mild exaggeration of the normal process, as with a somewhat overly seductive parent of the opposite sex or a sometimes absent same-sexed parent. Patients who had a basically negative relationship with a parent as a result of the parent's preference for a sibling or other real instances of rejection during the oedipal period do less well. Where there has been a severe distortion of the oedipal situation, as occurs, for example, when there is a death of a parent during the oedipal years, difficulties may also be anticipated.

SUMMARY

Patients selected for short-term anxiety-provoking psychotherapy are healthy, well-motivated people, eager to work hard in psychotherapy in order to gain an understanding of themselves and their problems. Some may wonder whether such ideal patients really exist. It is probably not a coincidence that Sifneos developed his technique in Boston, site of many colleges and universities, where students form a natural pool of patients for this therapy. The types of patients seen by Sifneos include those with anxiety attacks, moderately severe phobias, mild obsessive symptoms, and depressions. (Depressions are treated only when it is felt the symptoms are a response to an oedipal conflict.) More common than patients with symptoms are those with problems in interpersonal relationships. Indeed, these patients seem to do better in the treatment than those with pure symptomatic complaints. Examples are patients with problems in heterosexual relationships or with authority figures at work or in school. As with other forms of brief therapy discussed in this book, duration of illness and severity of symptoms are *not* criteria in themselves. It should not be thought that, because the patients selected are relatively healthy, they do not have real problems which cause them distress and which seriously interfere with their ability to get the most out of life. Examples of patients successfully treated by Sifneos include a 17-year-old college girl with severe examination anxiety and difficulty in accepting her feminine strivings; a 28-year-old housewife with a three-year history of anxiety, frigidity, and agoraphobia; and a 23-year-old woman who wanted help in ending her pattern of seeking out men who mistreated her.

THE OPENING PHASE OF THE TREATMENT

The treatment begins by utilizing the attitudes that have been evoked and encouraged during the evaluation interview. As a result, the patient expects to work hard at understanding himself or herself, expects the therapist to take an active role in helping to accomplish this task, and expects to be helped in the "brief" time that has been allotted. Thus the properly selected patient will bring high motivation and high expectations to the first session of the treatment. The therapist utilizes these factors and strives to maintain the treatment at a high level of intensity throughout.

The chief technique, and the technique that is most distinctive of this method of brief psychotherapy, is the use of anxiety-provoking confrontations. The most common example is the direct attack on the patient's defenses rather than attempts at interpreting the meaning or function of the defenses. Other aspects of the patient's productions or behavior may be challenged directly, sometimes in what seems to be a mocking or sarcastic manner. Thus, when a patient strays from the focus, when he or she avoids or disagrees with an interpretation, or when there is a general slack in the flow of material, the therapist is likely to confront the patient in a direct, forceful, challenging way. Behavioral manifestations of resistance such as lateness or missed appointments may be dealt with in a similar fashion.

An example of anxiety-provoking techniques used to keep the patient from continuing with pregenital issues follows.

PT: I am not feeling very well today, as I have told you already. I feel sick. I want you to do the talking for a while. I want something soothing today. After all, it's partly your fault that I'm feeling the way I do today. I'm achy, I have. . . .

TH (*interrupting*): And why is it my fault?

PT: Because you did not make an offer to give me another appointment after you canceled the one last week.

TH: We discussed all this before.

PT: Yes, I know, but you never offered to make up the time.

TH: If you wanted another appointment, why didn't you ask for one?

PT: You canceled it, so it was up to you to give me another one.

TH: What's going on today?

PT: I told you that I wanted to be soothed.

TH: I'm not going to soothe you, and you know better than that. Now, stop feeling sorry for yourself and let's get back to work.

PT (*sarcastic*): I don't feel like being self-inquisitive today.

TH: So, you are self-destructive today. Having had no hour last week, which you blame on me, now you are determined to waste this hour so as to be even with me. Now, what about all this appointment controversy?

PT: I told you that I wanted you to offer me another appointment.

TH: I know that. I also said that you could have asked for one if you wanted to. You are entitled to ask for what you want, in a mature way, but you are not entitled to act like a little spoiled child in here, because this is what we try to help you understand and overcome. Now, let me clarify something which I am sure you know only too well. I deal with you as a grownup person, not as a child, and furthermore, I am not here to play soothing games. Now, are you going to settle down and get to work, which you are perfectly capable of performing, as you have already demonstrated, or not? (Sifneos 1979, pp. 120–121)

The following is an example in which the therapist belittles the patient's defense of sadness and goes directly to the patient's wish to be given something. Note that at the end of this fragment the therapist helps to raise the patient's self-esteem by pointing out that the hurtful material really originated with the patient.

In his interview the patient told how he had spent all of his money and had gone out of his way to ask several of his friends for loans. He also complained of feeling weak, incapable of doing anything well, and of being "deflated" and sad. After hearing all this for a while, the doctor exclaimed, "You emphasize how sad you are, but we know you enjoy the attention you get from being broke, from begging, and from being helpless." "Good point," the patient said, and was silent for a while. He then added, "I understand, but you don't seem to care how I feel"; and then much more emphatically he went on, "You are so disinterested you don't give a damn. You don't give me a thing in the way of help."

DR: Like what, for example?
PT: Food for thought, anything, any old crumb.
DR: So. Although you profess to understand, you are right this minute, still begging, asking me to give, begging for crumbs.
PT (*pause*): Damn you!
DR: I can see you are angry when your manipulations fail. The question is whether begging for money and for bread crumbs . . . is to your best interest. Yet we do know you are capable at other times of getting along without all this self-pity.
PT: I know what you mean. I am surprised, however, that you do know all this.
DR: At this time you may interpret what I told you as having given you those bread crumbs. Actually I gave you back what *you told me* in our first interview.
PT: I had completely forgotten! (*He looked thoroughly surprised.*) (Sifneos 1972, p. 114)

The following example from the first session of a treatment illustrates anxiety-provoking techniques used to deal with acting out by the patient.

PT: I thought I should let you know that Bob and I had sexual intercourse last night for the first time. It was quite unsatisfactory.
TH (*taken aback, but trying to keep calm*): Can you tell me why?

PT: As you know, I did not want to have intercourse because I felt that if I did, I would have to marry Bob.

TH: Precisely!

PT: Yesterday, however, it seemed to me that now that I was starting therapy I would have the opportunity to discuss everything with my therapist, so I thought, "Why not give it a try?" What do you think? Was it wrong? I ask you as I would have asked my father if he were alive.

TH: It is not a matter of right and wrong. Furthermore, you are putting me in a position of judging whether what you did is to your advantage. It's not up to me to do this, but rather my role is to help you understand why you do what you do, and for you to decide accordingly.

PT: Yes, that's true.

TH: Well, not really, because although you decided to marry Bob you ask me what I think about it.

PT: But I haven't decided to marry him.

TH: Oh, yes you did. You told me [earlier in the session] that if you had sexual relations with him, and I quote you now, you "will be *forced* to marry Bob."

PT: Yes. I said that, but now I don't feel this way anymore.

TH: Maybe so, but your action seems to have taken precedence over your understanding. You had difficulty in deciding whether you should marry Bob or not which you wanted to examine during your therapy. Isn't that correct?

PT: Yes.

TH: So, you took the bull by the horns and decided that you are forced to marry him. I don't see that there is much for us to do in therapy anymore.

PT: Oh, no! You don't understand. I *do* want therapy. I *do* want to understand. Anyway, it was all very unsatisfactory. I felt that you would be my ally and help me out (*tremulously*), but . . . (*tears*). . . .

TH: Now you feel sorry for yourself!

PT: Well, yes. You're no help. You don't understand.

TH: Oh, yes, I do. You don't like what I say, but it's precisely because I want to help you out that I say what I said. Look here, forcing the issue does not solve the problem. Neither does making me the judge, like your father would have been, help you out. What is important is that we both try to understand your conflicts as well as your behavior. Do you want to do that?

PT: Oh, yes. Of course. That's why I'm here.

TH: Okay, then. (Sifneos 1979, pp. 82–83)

When taken out of context, as in the examples above, this technique often strikes observers as unnecessarily harsh and antitherapeutic. This impression is bolstered by Sifneos's own writings wherein he tends to emphasize the anxiety-provoking features of his treatment and to play down the anxiety-suppressing or supportive aspects of his techniques which are also an essential part of the therapeutic process. Interspersed with anxiety-provoking confrontations are supportive measures such as praising the patient for hard work and good insights. The feelings of helplessness and passivity which may be aroused by the anxiety-provoking statements are countered by frequent reminders that the patient is the one in control, is the one who is doing the work, and is the one who is really responsible for what happens during the course of the treatment. Frequent recapitulations and reformulations of what has been covered up to that point serve to provide a continuous intellectual framework which can be used by the patient to reassure himself or herself that he or she understands where the treatment is going, thus accentuating the patient's feeling of control over the process. Perhaps the most important of these supportive techniques is the use of the patient's material to provide the evidence for the interpretations and formulation. Staying close to the data provided by the patient allows the patient to see the source of the therapist's intervention, and he or she is thus able to participate actively in the therapeutic process. At the same time, staying with the data keeps the therapist from forcing "wild" or unwarranted interpretations onto the patient.

The following example of reassurance by the therapist occurs during a session in which the patient is recalling with much affect her feelings about seeing her father naked. The therapist is tying this material together with a dream the patient had previously presented in which the father had raped her.

TH: I know that all this is difficult.

PT: Yes (*giggling nervously*).

TH: You know the reason we're going into all this in so

much detail is because the sequence of all these events, pleasant and unpleasant, is very important. Now, shall we try to untangle all this a bit? (Sifneos 1979, p. 204)

THE ONGOING TREATMENT PROCESS

Just as the opening of the treatment is a continuation of the evaluation process, so the ongoing treatment is a continuation of the beginning of the treatment. The high level of tension and the activity of both therapist and patient continue throughout the treatment. In a successful therapy, this level of tension and activity will persist through the last session.

The aim of the therapist is to have the patient understand current symptoms or problems as the product of unresolved oedipal conflicts. By the end of the therapy this understanding should be both intellectual and emotional. The therapist generally starts by using events in the patient's current life situation to provide data for further exploration. By use of anxiety-provoking questions, the patient is then led to produce associations, memories, fantasies, and dreams that tie in the current material with significant material from the past. Similarly, when the material warrants it, the patient is pressed to relate feelings and thoughts about his or her current situation with feelings and thoughts about the therapist. Whenever possible the therapist shows the patient how his or her feelings for the therapist are similar to feelings toward significant figures from the past (the transference–parent link of Malan; see Chapter 6).

Here is an example, from the third session of a treatment, of the therapist linking the transference with both the husband and the father. Again, notice the therapist's confronting style.

PT: I haven't been honest with you, I gave you the wrong impression by telling you that I wanted to make all the decisions. I let you think the wrong thing and it bothered me that you got the wrong idea. I gave you the impression that I was an overbearing bitch with my husband.

DR: So you have some feelings about my impression of you?

The therapist here picks up the transference issue, since it was brought up also in the previous interview, and at that time he had not decided to pursue it.

PT: Maybe, but I don't want you to have ideas that are not true about me.

DR: You don't want me to! You mean I do not have the choice of deciding for myself?

PT (*blushing*): I suppose you have a point there. I never thought of it in this way.

DR: But isn't that what you do with your husband?

PT: I thought of it more in terms of my father. You see, at the time when my mother was away at the hospital, I used to stay in the house a lot, particularly at night after my sister had gone to bed. We used to play card games with my father; we had much fun; but I always told him what to do, and he always did exactly what I wanted.

DR: So, as you were the boss with your father and with your husband, now you want to be the boss with me, here. (Sifneos 1972, pp. 152–153)

As with other forms of psychotherapy, there will be periods when the treatment is flowing smoothly and periods of resistance. When the patient is working well, the main task of the therapist is to keep the material on the focus. Through his or her activity the therapist participates as a partner in helping the patient to understand his or her conflicts. The therapist often recapitulates and may praise the patient for the work he or she is doing. When the material warrants it, the therapist will offer interpretations, giving the patient a new way of understanding the material with which he or she has been working. The therapist will point out to the patient, should the patient fail to see it, when material relating to the focus applies to the patient–therapist relationship.

When periods of resistance appear, the therapist will become even more active. Most commonly the resistance, in the form of the diminution of the patient's flow of material, can be related to transference issues, and this should be interpreted to the patient. Thus it can be seen that transference interpretations are used for two different, though related, functions. One is to revivify the oedipal conflict and make it more meaningful to the patient, and the other is to help overcome resistance. In neither of these uses of the transference is it necessary or desirable to wait for negative feelings to emerge; both positive and negative aspects of the transference can be interpreted as early as the material warrants which, as has been seen, can occur even during the evaluation interview.

Resistance can also be attacked directly. Sifneos believes that with patients selected according to his criteria there is no danger in overwhelming the defenses by pointing out the underlying impulses directly. Over the course of several sessions, he will reiterate the same point until the patient finally acknowledges it, not only intellectually but also emotionally, and then confirms the point with the production of new and relevant material in the form of hitherto unknown memories or fantasies. Most important to this technique is that the therapist have the data from material presented by the patient to justify the interpretation or confrontation with which he or she is pounding the patient. As Sifneos has said, "pounding patients with a truth produces good results" (Davanloo 1978, p. 241). (The corollary is probably also correct; that is, pounding patients with material that is not "true" produces bad results.) When the data warrant it, interpretations can be made on a very deep level, as long as they stay within the oedipal focus and do not involve preoedipal issues. Thus interpretations dealing directly with incestuous wishes and castration anxiety can be made with some patients. Similarly, murderous wishes toward parents or siblings can also be interpreted.

In the following example, direct incestuous material becomes available after the therapist points out the patient's slip. Note how at the end of the fragment the therapist refers to the patient's capacity to understand herself as a means of helping her to achieve mastery over the material.

    PT: Maybe my father was right. My father was so good to me and I took such good care of him when my mother was in the hospital, but I'm not a good wife to fath. . . .
    DR: To your *father*?
    PT (*blushing*): Oh, My God, I meant to say my husband.
    DR: Yes, I know, but you said father.
    PT: I guess so if that's what I said—
    DR: You mean you have forgotten?

PT: Well, no.

DR: That is exactly what you said, even if you did not exactly finish the word, so what about it?

PT: You know what I mean.

DR: No. As a matter of fact, let us try to see what you've been telling me today. You talked about the same queer feeling that you had when you saw me in the corridor talking with a blonde as you had for Bill. You talked about sexual thoughts and about your doubts in reference to your husband. Finally, you talked—by mistake, of course!—about being a good wife to your *father*. Now let us look at what all this means.

The therapist by recapitulating focuses the patient's attention on the underlying sexual wishes for her father.

PT (*still blushing*): I guess I must have had some feelings of that kind, way back then. I remember now. When my mother was in the hospital I used to cook for my father and he used to say, "You cook so well, you cook better than your mother." And I would get that warm feeling inside like being a wife to him.

DR: So you see that some of the feelings that you have for other men are the same that you had for your father at that time; but, for one reason or another, you seem to exclude your husband. Why is that?

PT: Only since the time my mother died. Up to that time, as I told you, everything was all right between us.

DR: I know, but do you think that maybe your mother's death had something to do with your wanting to be a wife to your father?

PT (*pauses for a long time and then says*): God forbid, not in *that* way, I never thought of it. (*Seeming to be very upset, finally.*) I don't want to think about it.

DR: It's time you thought about it, if you want to understand yourself. (Sifneos 1972, pp. 160–161)

Because of the need for accurate information, Sifneos strongly recommends that the therapist take notes throughout the treatment. He suggests that the therapist review these notes prior to each session. Because of the intensity and rapidity of the flow of the material during a session, the therapist does not have the time to try to recollect previous events unless he or she is well prepared. When the patient fails to recollect previous material, reading back the patient's own words often has a powerful emotional impact.

All the modalities of psychotherapy, including working with dreams and fantasies, are used in this technique. There is not sufficient time to fully analyze a dream, but the patient or therapist may pick out one aspect of the material to concentrate on. Often the most useful function of a dream or a fantasy is to confirm to both patient and therapist that the work is progressing correctly.

As the treatment progresses, the patient's relationship with parents and other significant figures in his or her past will become clearer. The therapist uses this data to help the patient modify relationships with significant people in his or her current life as well as his or her interactions with the therapist. Often the therapist takes a direct educational stance, pointing out to the patient how, because of his or her new understanding of the origin of his or her fears, different and more adaptive modes of behavior in his or her current life can now be employed. The patient is encouraged to try out some of these new ways of behaving during the course of therapy. At the same time the patient is taught how to employ the techniques of treatment, that is, to understand the origin of previous patterns of behavior and to use this understanding to change those patterns, so that work on problems may continue after the treatment has formally ended. Thus the treatment provides a learning experience for the patient which can be used to solve new problems in the future.

TERMINATION

The attitude presented to the patient in the evaluation interview and throughout the treatment sets the stage for a relatively rapid and atraumatic termination. The patient is told at the beginning of the treatment that the therapy will be short term. No definite number of sessions is set, and there is, therefore, no fixed termination date. When the patient asks how long short term is, Sifneos states, "It's going to be up to you to solve your problem in whatever time limit you want, but it will be for a few months only" (Davanloo 1978, p. 331).

Thus, right from the beginning, the therapist lets the patient know that it is part of the patient's responsibility to decide when to terminate. This helps to reduce the patient's feelings of passivity and dependence throughout the treatment and prepares him or her to initiate termination. In actuality, about half the patients initiate termination themselves, and in the other half of the cases termination is initiated by the therapist. Sifneos's statistics reveal that 90 percent of his completed cases last 12 to 16 sessions, while 10 percent last 16 to 20. None has gone beyond 20 sessions.

Termination usually occurs after the patient has achieved intellectual and emotional awareness of the underlying conflict, has shown evidence of change in behavior in his or her current life situation, and has shown the ability to utilize the knowledge gained in therapy to solve new problems encountered during the course of treatment. While this may sound overly ambitious, these goals are attainable when using the correct techniques with properly selected patients. The most important task of the therapist to facilitate termination is the diligent avoidance of all pregenital issues throughout the treatment process. Sifneos believes that if pregenital issues are avoided, there will be no intense separation anxiety, and, therefore, separation will not be an important therapeutic issue that must be resolved. Usually one or two sessions are scheduled after termination has been agreed upon, but they generally continue the pattern of the previous sessions, continuing to focus on the oedipal conflict. The avoidance of pregenital issues not only makes separation issues less important, but also makes the development of a transference neurosis less likely. A fully developed transference neurosis would, of course, make separation impossible without extensive further treatment. The selection of patients, the brevity of the treatment, the sharing of responsibility of the treatment with the patient, and the avoidance of pregenital issues all make the development of a transference neurosis extremely unlikely.

Most patients are able to end treatment and maintain the positive feelings about the therapist and the treatment that prevailed throughout most of the therapy. The sense of accomplishment that the patient feels at having understood important things about himself or herself and at the changes he or she has seen occur allows the patient to leave the treatment with relatively little ambivalence. Careful attention to the patient's actual changes in behavior, thinking, and affect is necessary so that the therapist can evaluate the genuineness of the patient's improvement.

Sifneos does not mention the problem of those who require further treatment after 20 sessions have been completed. He does state that some of the patients he has followed over time required further treatment at a later date. If a patient does require continuing treatment, it implies that there has been an error in selection and diagnosis. If this is noted early in the course of treatment, the treatment can be modified to meet the patient's needs, or the patient can be transferred to another therapist. If it becomes evident only at the time of termination that the patient requires further treatment, it is probably best to transfer the patient to a different therapist. Since a long-term treatment would not use the anxiety-provoking techniques of this therapy, a shift of treatment technique would probably be difficult for both patient and therapist.

Sifneos has provided extensive clinical material, including many verbatim examples of his work, so that the reader can get an excellent picture of his entire technique from his published work (Davanloo 1978; Sifneos 1972, 1979).

COUNTERTRANSFERENCE ISSUES

It would seem that the most prominent countertransference problem to arise from short-term anxiety-provoking psychotherapy would be the mobilization of the therapist's sadism through the use of the confronting techniques. Sifneos has not found this to be a problem. Indeed, he feels that reaction–formation to the sadistic impulses is a more prevalent issue, leading to a holding back by the therapist. Thus the therapist will not fully utilize the anxiety-provoking techniques and will not confront the patient adequately, with the result that the treatment will not move forward as rapidly and as thoroughly as it might. Nevertheless, the danger that the therapist might use the technique to establish power over the patient or to degrade and humiliate him or her in the service of being "anxiety-provoking" must be kept in mind at all times by people using this technique and by those selecting others for training in this method. For similar reasons it is important in selecting patients that particular attention be paid to the patient's masochistic trends. While Sifneos presents a successfully treated woman who sought out men who mistreated her, he could demonstrate that this pattern of behavior was related to an oedipal conflict. When the masochistic behavior is more characterological, this technique is probably contraindicated, even if the patient meets the other selection criteria, because anxiety-provoking attempts to stay within the focus would be experienced by the patient as gratification of the masochism, leading to a therapeutic impasse.

A frequent problem occurs when the therapist has difficulty in balancing the anxiety-provoking and the anxiety-suppressive aspects of the treatment. Some therapists will offer unnecessary or too frequent reassurances, while others will not offer sufficient support to enable the patient to maximize the benefits of the treatment. The proper balance obviously needs to be individualized for each patient, but the tension should be maintained at a fairly high level, certainly higher than for most other forms of psychotherapy.

Difficulties will also occur if the therapist fails to keep the patient within the focus. As with most forms of brief psychotherapy, it is tempting for the therapist to explore various side issues as the patient is working so well and could obviously provide interesting material in many areas of interest to the therapist. While this may gratify the therapist's curiosity, it would seriously undermine the treatment, for not only would time be taken from working on the focus, but, more importantly, working on preoedipal issues with the intensity inherent in this treatment modality would cause the transference to deepen rapidly so that successful separation would not be possible in the allotted time. Similarly, if the therapist does not recognize the optimum time for termination, the therapy will continue inevitably into preoedipal issues, again making separation impossible within the brief therapy framework.

Other difficulties will arise if the therapist, either because of excessive therapeutic zeal or because of lack of skill, makes errors in the selection procedure. If there is any doubt as to the suitability of a patient for this method of treatment, another evaluation, preferably by another therapist, should be done. The need for accurate evaluation and selection of patients for this technique cannot be overemphasized. The combination of repeated attacks on a patient's defenses and the use of psychodynamically deep interpretations could lead to serious damage in vulnerable individuals. While no such cases have been reported, an acute psychotic episode or a severe depression with suicidal potential is possible if this technique is used with inappropriate patients.

RESULTS

Sifneos has conducted a number of follow-up studies, with some patients interviewed as much as four years after treatment. Because of methodological problems, the results are not meaningful statistically, but a clear picture emerges of the results of the treatment. Most patients regarded the therapy as a positive experience and retained their positive feelings for the therapist. While few symptoms disappeared outright, there was a frequent diminution in their intensity, and patients felt the symptoms to be less incapacitating. More striking than the changes in symptoms was an oft-reported increase in self-esteem, which the patients attributed to the treatment. The patients had also learned new ways of dealing with problems during the course of the therapy and were able to apply these new techniques to other problems that they encountered during the follow-up period. Sifneos gives an example of a woman who developed the symptom of overeating after the end of therapy. With much effort, and on her own, she was able to "analyze" the meaning of the symptom and relate it to early memories of comforting by her mother. This was followed by the patient's realizing how much she missed her mother, with the release of much affect. The overeating subsided. Often there was an improvement in interpersonal relationships. In some patients, dynamic changes manifested by changes in the patient's defenses to a more mature or adaptive level were noted.

TEACHING SHORT-TERM
ANXIETY-PROVOKING PSYCHOTHERAPY

Sifneos originally taught his technique to senior residents in psychiatry. He found considerable resistance, in part because the residents had learned and were committed to techniques of long-term therapy. At the present time he trains only volunteers, people who wish to work with him on an elective, not a required, basis, and he prefers to work with people early in their training. The selection of the patient, that is, the evaluation interview, is done by the supervisor. Thereafter, the patient is seen by the student who reports to the supervisor weekly. Note taking is stressed so that the supervisor gets as accurate a picture of the treatment as possible. At times videotapes are used.

The resistance to learning this technique which Sifneos experienced has been noted by others. The stance of the therapist doing anxiety-provoking therapy is the exact opposite of what most therapists are taught to do. Most therapists spend their time trying to *reduce* anxiety, not to increase it. Most are trained to respect and interpret defenses, not to try to assault them; and most therapists are taught that it takes a long time before deep genetic interpretations should be made. Sifneos, by emphasizing the anxiety-provoking aspect of his treatment, tends to foster these resistances. It is certainly true that this technique is not for all therapists. It requires an active, energetic therapist, with a great deal of self-confidence, but if the selection criteria and technique are followed carefully, it can be a safe and most efficient therapeutic modality.

SUMMARY

Short-term anxiety-provoking psychotherapy is a brief psychotherapy approach which, through a combination of careful selection procedures and an aggressive technique, permits the exploration of oedipal conflicts in a short period of time. Patients selected must have a high degree of motivation, superior intelligence, psychological awareness, and an absence of serious psychopathology, including the absence of serious characterological disorders. The patient must have an oedipal conflict as the basis of his or her symptomatology. The anxiety-provoking aspect of the technique consists of frequent confrontations of the patient by the therapist, with direct attacks on the defenses rather than interpretations of them. When this technique is successful, the patient will produce sufficient material in the form of memories, dreams, and fantasies to permit the reconstruction of the original oedipal conflict. This will be followed by changes in the patient's relationships with people in his or her current life and will be seen in changes in the transference. When there is both an intellectual and an emotional understanding of the conflict, and when changes in the patient's current life have occurred, the therapy is terminated without much attention to termination issues. Ninety percent of the treatments last from 12 to 16 sessions; none go beyond 20 sessions. The chief countertransference problems with this technique occur as a result of the therapist's being too aggressive with the patient or from a reaction–formation to the aggression, leading to an avoidance of confrontation on the part of the therapist.

5

THE TIME-LIMITED
PSYCHOTHERAPY
OF MANN

THE PSYCHOLOGICAL DEVELOPMENT
OF THE SENSE OF TIME

James Mann is interested in the concept of time. The opening chapter of his first book (Mann 1973) is an elegant review of the meaning of time, its psychological development, and its place in the history of psychotherapy. Mann points out that little has been written about time in relation to psychotherapy and that the subject is usually avoided during most forms of psychotherapy. Time is intimately connected with mortality and other unpleasant limitations of the human condition; so it is unconsciously avoided by both therapist and patient. The reason can be found in the developmental history of the sense of time.

The earliest sense of time in infancy accompanies the feelings of fusion with the mother and is consonant with the sense of omnipotence characteristic of that phase of development. It is really a sense of timelessness rather than a sense of time per se. That is, all things are felt to be possible; time is experienced as infinite, without beginning or end. This is the sense of time that persists in the unconscious and that is

familiar to therapists working with unconscious material. With
the development of feelings of separation and the awareness
of an external reality, the sense of real time in contrast to
infinite time begins to be formed. One of the universal developmental tasks, which no one masters completely, is to
recognize and accept that time is indeed finite and that, therefore, everyone is mortal and has to die, leaving many wishes
unfulfilled. Mann reviews data showing that the sense of real
time develops simultaneously with the sense of reality. Indeed, it can be said that time is one of the chief measures we
use to distinguish reality from unreality. However, infinite
time continues to exert its obvious appeal throughout life,
manifesting itself in dreams, fantasies, and altered states of
consciousness.

Mann's time-limited psychotherapy depends on the inherent conflict between real and infinite time and utilizes the
pressure of the infinite time sense to express itself. The therapy provides an environment in which there can be an experi-
ential recapitulation of the normal maturational stages of the
sense of time. Initially, the sense of infinite time and omnipotence is recreated; then there is a period of ambivalence
where there is a struggle with the realities and limits of time,
followed by a period of separation which is experienced and
accepted in a more adaptive manner than was achieved during the actual childhood of the patient. It is possible to recreate these phenomena in the treatment because of the formal
arrangements of the therapy: the time limit, the focus on a
"central issue," the technique of the therapist, and the selection of the patient.

THE FIXED TIME LIMIT OF TWELVE SESSIONS

The most innovative of Mann's contributions is the setting
of a fixed and rigid time limit for the therapy. Although Rank
had experimented with this approach, he later abandoned it,
and it was not until Mann started his therapy in 1964 that this
idea took hold. It has now been accepted by Malan and some
other workers. Mann feels that it is only by setting a fixed time
limit that the ambiguity about ending treatment that exists in
so many current psychotherapies can be eliminated. This ambiguity is used as a defense by both patient and therapist in

order to avoid confronting the inevitability of separation and death. As a result of the unconscious resistance to termination, the majority of long-term psychotherapies do not end with a planned and mutually agreed-upon termination but, rather, are ended either by a move on the part of the patient or therapist, by reality factors such as changes in schedules or finances, or, most commonly, by the patient or therapist as a result of unconscious transference or countertransference issues which have not emerged in the treatment. Therapies that end as a result of these issues, especially those that end because of transference or countertransference impasses, usually are terminated without adequate working through of the separation. A fixed time limit forces both therapist and patient to confront the issue of termination with a minimum of evasion.

On the basis of his own extensive clinical experience with psychotherapy, Mann arbitrarily picked 12 sessions as the duration for his therapy. He states that 10 or 14 sessions might work just as well as 12, but there is merit in keeping the number standardized at 12 so that treatments can be compared more easily with one another. There is an initial evaluation, which can last up to 4 sessions, and which is not counted in the 12 sessions. (If the therapy is done by the same therapist who does the evaluation, the session where the patient agrees to the treatment plan and the actual therapeutic work begins is counted as the first session.) Those patients who are found suitable for time-limited psychotherapy are then treated for 12 sessions, usually spaced one a week. Except where external circumstances, for example, an impending move, dictate otherwise, sessions should not be scheduled more frequently than once a week. If appointments have to be missed because of illness or other unavoidable circumstances, the sessions are made up, preferably without changing the original termination date.

THE CENTRAL ISSUE

After the evaluation, and once the patient has been found suitable for time-limited psychotherapy, the therapist presents the focus or, in Mann's terminology, the central issue, to the patient for his or her agreement, with the understanding that the central issue can be modified as the treatment goes on. (If the evaluation is performed by someone other than the treating therapist, the therapist makes the formulation of the central issue during the first session.) The central issue should reflect a theme that connects the presenting symptoms with other difficulties experienced in the past and with conflicts in the patient's childhood that can be seen by the therapist to be dynamically related to the current problems. It is thus apparent that as complete a psychodynamic understanding of the patient as possible should be made during the initial evaluation; hence there is no time limit on the evaluation sessions. Because putting the central issue in terms of either the original impulse or the most prominent defenses against the impulse will call forth resistance, it is most effective, and most economical, to put the central issue in terms of some conscious feeling which the patient will acknowledge as meaningful. If skillfully selected, the patient will not only acknowledge the feeling but will also feel understood by the therapist in an emotional way, thus furthering the sense of the therapist's omnipotence that is characteristic of the first phase of the treatment. Examples of a central issue are:

> I gather from all that you have told me that the greatest problem facing you at this time is your very deep disappointment with yourself to find yourself as you are at this time in your life. (Mann 1973, p. 18)

> Because there have been a number of sudden and very painful events in your life, things always seem uncertain, and you are excessively nervous because you do not expect anything to go along well. Things are always uncertain for you. (Mann 1973, p. 20)

> Although you are a big man physically and although you are successful in your work, you have long been plagued by the fear of helplessness if you are left alone. (Mann and Goldman 1982, p. 65)

> You have always given of yourself to so many others and yet you feel and always have felt both undeserving and unrewarded. (Mann and Goldman 1982, p. 84)

It can be seen that the central issue reflects painful feelings that the patient has had about himself or herself over a long period of time. It is thus a way of addressing negative aspects of the patient's sense of self, that is, the sense of his or her own inadequacy. One of the goals of the treatment is to enable the patient to discover the cause of these painful feelings and in so doing gain a more positive sense of self. It requires considerable empathy on the part of the therapist to determine those feelings which speak most directly to the patient's sense of self (Mann and Goldman 1982).

The formulation of the central issue is put in derivative terms; that is, the feelings forming the central issue are not primary affects such as anger, but rather defensive feelings such as disappointment or uncertainty. The statement of the formulation tends to be understanding and nonconfronting. As will be seen later, these characteristics of the central issue set the tone for the entire therapy.

While the central issue sets the tone for the treatment, it is the definiteness of the termination date that provides the shape. After the patient has agreed to work on the central issue the therapist tells the patient that he or she will be seen for 12 sessions and that the therapy will end on a specific date which is given to the patient. Once again the patient is asked to agree with this treatment plan.

THE FIRST PHASE—A RETURN
TO TIMELESSNESS

Because the therapist implicitly or explicitly states that he or she is going to help the patient in a relatively brief period of time, the patient's feelings of omnipotence, that anything is possible, are quickly reawakened, allowing the patient to return to an earlier stage of development where the sense of timelessness was prevalent. Thus, the first phase of the treatment, usually comprising the first 3 to 4 sessions, shows a rapid amelioration of symptoms, with much positive feeling for the therapist and a large outpouring of clinically significant historical material. In order to encourage this initial phase, it is essential that the therapist believe, and convey to the patient that he or she believes, that he or she can help the patient in the 12 sessions allotted. Thus, when patients ask, as they frequently do, whether there will be enough time for them to get help with their problems in the allotted time, the answer must be an unequivocal yes.

In addition to the phenomena resulting from the patient's belief that anything is possible, the first phase of the treatment is characterized by a release of feelings resulting from the sympathetic exploration of the central issue. This abreaction promotes positive transference feelings and the rapid development of a therapeutic alliance, which in turn contributes to the decrease in symptomatology that is seen during this phase of the treatment.

During the first phase of the treatment the therapist is an empathic listener; there is usually little need to make interpretations at this time. The patient's progress is actively encouraged. The positive transference is generally not interpreted. The main task of the therapist is to keep the treatment focused on the central issue, and most of his or her interventions are directed toward this end. The patient reexperiences the "golden glow" of the childhood omnipotence and would like to talk about and resolve all possible issues, thus setting the stage for the first conflict with the therapist. As the therapist repeatedly brings the patient back to the central issue, it becomes apparent to the patient that not all issues will be dealt with. In this way the patient is confronted with reality. At the same time, the sessions are passing, and the patient becomes aware (though perhaps not consciously so at this stage) of the passage of time. These two factors, the insistence of the therapist on staying with the central issue and the passage of time, lead to the loss of the golden glow and to the beginnings of the ambivalence characteristic of the second phase of treatment. It can be seen that, if the therapist is seduced by the patient into working on various side issues, the reality of the treatment situation will become lost and the treatment will not develop successfully.

The beginning of treatment is also used to educate the patient, particularly about psychological phenomena of which the patient may be unaware. For example, from the second treatment session:*

---

* This excerpt, and the following clinical excerpts in this chapter, are taken from a case presented in great detail in Mann's book. The transcript not only illustrates all aspects of Mann's technique, but it is also an interesting and very moving record of a psychotherapeutic experience.

DR: Sometimes there are things that bother us and we are not really aware of what they are. They are somewhere inside us. We don't know what they are, and we need help to find out what they are. (Mann 1973, p. 102)

THE SECOND PHASE—THE REEMERGENCE OF REALITY

Much of the interpretive work of the therapy occurs during the second stage. Resistances begin to appear which can be interpreted to the patient in relation to the genetics of his or her conflicts as well as in their transference manifestations. The patient will produce material indicating how his or her conflicts are affecting the current life situation, and again genetic and transference interpretations can be made, always remaining within the framework of the central issue. Frequently there will be a return of symptoms with discouragement about the treatment and disappointment in the therapist. While the therapist understands that much of what is happening with the patient is the result of his or her struggle with the limitations of time and thereby with the limitations of reality, it is rarely necessary or useful to interpret this directly to the patient. The treatment really proceeds simultaneously on two levels. The manifest level is the patient and therapist working psychotherapeutically to understand and clarify the central issue as it relates to the past, the present, and the therapist. While this work is being done, the phases of treatment, as outlined here, occur, usually without the patient's awareness. Thus, during the first phase of treatment the patient will not report a general sense of well-being and euphoria but will tell of events that took place during the week that will indicate an improvement in functioning. So too, the discouragement and ambivalence of the second phase will come out in the reporting of specific events which were distressing to the patient, as well as through behavior in the sessions, for example, lateness. The accompanying affect often must be brought out by the therapist. To concretize and emphasize the passage of time, Mann usually asks sometime during the middle of the treatment how many sessions are left. The answer is often vague or incorrect, highlighting the patient's need to preserve an ambiguity about the end of the treatment.

The following fragment from the fifth session is characteristic of the interchanges of the middle phase of the treatment.

PT: I guess I don't like to displease anybody. That's
my way, and I don't know if I change. I just don't like
to hurt people.

DR: You mean that if you don't do as you think I want
you to do that I will be hurt.

PT: I feel you are giving up time to try and help me.
At least I could try and help myself.

DR: Well, that is certainly a very helpful way for you to
look at it. But who are you going to do it for. For you? Or
in order not to hurt me?

PT: No, for myself.

DR: You're sure now.

PT: Mmmm. Because I feel that's what you want me to
do—for myself.

DR: Not for me.

PT: I figure that if I am displeasing you, it's still connected with me because I am not doing what I should do
for myself. You are not being hurt by it, but I am probably
hurting myself.

DR: Except that you would be afraid that you might be
hurting me.

PT: Not really. Wasting your time. You try to help me,
and I should try to help myself—which I have been trying
to do.

DR: That's certainly true. But it's very difficult for you to
displease. What's going to happen if you find yourself in a
position here where you will have to say no to me for
one reason or another?

PT: Maybe as time goes on, I am hoping to get that
courage and demand to say to somebody eventually—

DR: It takes courage.

PT: Everything that I have been asked of I have been
able to fulfill. There will be a day when I probably won't
be able to, and I will have to say no. I hope I have the
courage to say no when the time comes.

DR: You say that it takes courage to say no. That means
you are afraid.

PT: I am not always afraid to say no. Like I mentioned last week, if I feel that I can't do something, then I can say no. If I don't say no, it's because I feel I can do it, so why not do it. But then I have a voice behind me saying, "You don't want to do it, what are you doing it for?" I just don't want to say no. It isn't a fear. I can't explain it. If I make somebody happy, then I am happy myself.

DR: Where did you learn this from—this whole idea of trying to make everybody happy?

PT: I don't know. It wasn't at home.

DR: It wasn't at home.

PT: No. I never saw anybody put themselves out of their way to make anything extra happy. What everybody did they had to do, and that was it. (Mann 1973, pp. 127–128)

The patient then goes on to talk in a very meaningful way about the family constellation during the time she was growing up. The mother was hypercritical and very demanding of the patient and her sisters, while whatever the brothers did was accepted.

THE THIRD PHASE—TERMINATION

It is during the third phase of treatment, the end of the therapy, that the two levels of the treatment come together. Separation is a universal experience and plays some role in every conflict; so it is possible in every case to relate some aspect of the central issue to the actual ending of the treatment. The termination issue must be dealt with explicitly no later than the tenth session. This is often as difficult for the therapist as it is for the patient. This phase of the treatment is usually an emotionally rich experience for both participants. The therapist continues to focus on the central issue, now relating it as much as possible to the feelings in the transference as the treatment comes to an end, paying particular attention to the negative affects that are uncovered. Mann believes the separation experience is essential for the therapeutic results of his treatment. "Active and appropriate management of the termination will allow the patient to internalize the therapist as a replacement or substitute for the earlier ambivalent object. This time the internalization will be more positive (never totally so), less anger-laden, and less guilt-laden, thereby making separation a genuine maturational event" (Mann 1973, p. 36).

While emphasizing the importance of the termination experience, Mann disclaims a similarity between what happens in his treatment and what Alexander called the corrective emotional experience (see Chapter 3). Mann interprets Alexander too narrowly, and what Mann describes as new internalizations, as a result of experiencing the separation conflict with the therapist, seems identical with the phenomenon that Alexander was calling the corrective emotional experience. Whatever the mechanism may prove to be, it is clear that a profound experience which can have lasting ramifications in all areas of a person's life can occur as a result of a brief encounter.

The following fragment from the 11th session is typical of the termination phase.

DR: How many times do we have?

PT: Left? One.

DR: How do you feel about that?

PT: I don't know. I was thinking about that yesterday. To me it feels as if I was going to school.

DR: Oh, you were thinking about it yesterday?

PT: Yesterday. Thursday night when I was going to school. I went to ceramics, and I was thinking of coming here Friday, and I said "Gee, that's just like going to school when you are going to graduate but—that—it doesn't bother me."

DR: But graduations sometimes are kind of a bothering period in life. What does graduation mean to you?

PT: Like when you are all through school—college— and you have achieved so much schooling. Not that I have achieved something.

DR: What else does graduation mean?

PT: That's all I can think of.

DR: You finish school and achieve a certain amount or kind of education, and what follows?

PT: Oh, you have to work when you graduate from

school. You have to go out and get a job and work out what you've learned and take over yourself.

DR: Go on your own.

PT: Mmmm. And I try to figure things out.

DR: Do you have any qualms about that—after next week you will be on your own?

PT: Just be more or less wondering how things will be, but I just have to wait to find out.

DR: But you do have these wonderings.

PT: I have to have that, I think.

DR: You say you would have to have that. I am not going to flunk you in this course.

PT: Well, I couldn't really sit here and say, "Oh, I am going to be fine after next week."

DR: I want you to say exactly what you feel.

PT: I found out a lot of things about myself, and now I feel I can handle them probably myself.

DR: But you have your qualms.

PT: Yeah. I am still wondering if I will still be able to handle it the way I can handle it now.

DR: Next week you will get your diploma. You will graduate this school. You will be on your own, and that's okay by you, but you sometimes wonder whether—

PT: I will be able to make it. I'll make it. I know that I am not going to feel that much better just because I am not coming back but—

DR: Wait. Tell me that again.

PT: I mean coming every week. I feel I come every week, and I am getting help—help—and it helps me out till the following week. So I am not going to be all better, as if I had a cold and the next week it's going to be gone, because I am all through coming. What is bothering me will still be there—just have to work it out myself—that's how I feel right now.

DR: Do you think that you will miss coming here?

PT: Probably if I get a spell or something. I will be looking forward to help, but I will have to do that myself.

DR: You think that only if you get a spell or something that you will think about and wish you were coming here.

PT: If I feel I need—

DR: You said you feel good. Do you think you will miss seeing me?

PT: No. I don't think that I will miss coming here. Like I said last week.

DR: I didn't say coming here.

PT: I like your company and everything, but I don't think I will miss you that way.

DR: Are you telling me the cold honest truth?

PT: I don't know how to put it.

DR: Just put it very simply, honestly.

PT: No. I just as soon not have to come. If I don't feel well, I am not going to sit there and say, "I wish I could go to see Dr. Mann." Instead I will probably put on my coat and go out. I hope that's how I feel, anyway.

DR: That's very good.

PT: That's how I am looking forward to feeling.

DR: I can tell the way you were smiling that you like seeing me.

PT: Like I said to my husband—he asked how I was making out and everything—what seems important to me, everybody in the family will think it is so minor that it shouldn't be bothering me, but you would listen to me. I told him that's what I liked about coming. Things that seem important to me seem important to you.

DR: Yes. (Mann 1973, pp. 173–174)

During the termination phase there is sometimes a re-emergence of symptoms as well as occasional acting out of separation issues. When these phenomena occur they must of course be interpreted as resistances to dealing with separation directly in the therapy. When the patient expresses doubt that he or she will be able to end the treatment in the allotted time, the therapist must remain firm in the belief that no further treatment is needed. If the patient asks what to do if symptoms continue or return, the best answer is "you will know what to do." This serves to convey the confidence of the therapist in the treatment and in the capacity of the patient to deal with whatever issues will arise.

In fact, Mann has only on rare occasions extended the length of the treatment. This has happened when some traumatic event has occurred during the course of the therapy, for example, a death, which requires time to assimilate and also which will necessarily stir up additional material relevant to the central issue. Mann states that in his experience he has not seen psychotic decompensations or major depressions developing during the course of time-limited psychotherapy. If these events were to occur, other forms of therapy would obviously be required. On rare occasions, Mann has seen patients for a few additional sessions some weeks after termination to conclude the work of separation when this has not been done adequately in the allotted time. In general, if it appears at the time of termination that additional therapy is needed, it is preferable, whenever possible, to allow the patient a period without therapy to see if he or she cannot consolidate the gains of the therapy after the active phase of the teatment has ended.

SELECTION OF PATIENTS

One of the great advantages of Mann's technique is its wide applicability. Whereas other brief therapy techniques have strict selection criteria, his technique is available to most people coming for treatment. He excludes only the actively psychotic and those so severely depressed as to be incapable of working in the treatment. He also excludes those "whose desperation in life centers exclusively around the need for and the incapacity to tolerate object relations" (Mann 1973, p. 74). This would exclude most borderline patients. In addition, the finding of a central issue and the patient's agreement with it are essential to the treatment. Thus, those patients who present a vague picture, either of symptoms or of their past, would not be suitable, nor would those patients who are unable to decide to work on any specific central issue be accepted for treatment.

In a more recent book, Mann and Goldman (1982) have tried to expand on the above selection criteria. Evaluation of the patient's ego-strength is important. It can often be measured by the history of success in work and in forming relationships. Most important for successful time-limited psychotherapy is the capacity of the patient for rapid effective engagement and disengagement. Patients with certain clinical syndromes usually have difficulties in these areas. The schizoid patient will have trouble forming relationships; certain obsessional patients cannot engage their feelings rapidly; some hysterics will not accept a 12-session limit or may not be able to remain focused on the central issue; some patients with strong dependency needs will resist the treatment because of their fear of loss; some narcissistic patients will not accept a 12-session limit; some depressive characters will not be able to form a rapid therapeutic alliance; and some patients with psychosomatic disorders have never successfully tolerated loss. Mann concludes that his selection criteria are still not perfected and that clinical assessment and judgment are requried to decide which patients will be suitable for time-limited psychotherapy.

While people of all age groups (excluding children) have been treated with time-limited psychotherapy, Mann feels his technique is particularly suitable for young people in middle or late adolescence, that is, the college years. The conflicts of these years tend to center on problems of independence versus dependence, thus reviving the earlier separation–individuation conflicts. In this group it is important for the development of age-appropriate behavior that independence be encouraged. Time-limited psychotherapy is attractive to the patient in that the brief course reinforces these desires to be independent. At the same time, the termination phase of the treatment can serve as a consolidating and growth-enhancing experience, while the dependency needs that are also active at this age are not reinforced as they would be by an open-ended or long-term therapy.

Another group particularly suited for this treatment is people who are psychologically unsophisticated and nonintrospective, including many working-class people and people from lower socioeconomic classes. There is no requirement that patients selected for this treatment respond meaningfully to trial interpretations, in contrast to the requirements of many of the other techniques. The central issue, speaking directly to the feelings of the patient, permits the formation of a rapid therapeutic alliance without much intellectual awareness being required of the patient. The supportive and educational stance of the therapist allows him or her to teach these patients some of the basic concepts of psychological functioning as the treatment proceeds (see excerpt on page 86). The positive transference present during the first phase of the treatment permits this educational process to proceed rapidly, free from the usual resistance present when one adult is being taught by another adult. In addition, the "prescription" of 12 sessions is consonant with most people's experience with medical doctors, that is, "take these pills for 12 days," so that psychotherapy with a fixed time limit is often perceived as less unfamiliar and hence less threatening than open-ended psychotherapy by those who have had little or no previous experience with psychological treatments.

Examples of patients treated successfully by Mann in 12 sessions include a 30-year-old graduate student presenting with feelings of lack of self-confidence, feelings of "drifting without motivation," anxiety attacks, and multiple somatic complaints; a 29-year-old woman, separated after a 2-year marriage which was not consummated sexually, who had a long history of difficulty in her relationships with men; a 39-year-old working-class mother of six with a 10-year history of anxiety attacks and increasingly disabling phobic symptoms; and a 54-year-old woman from a poor rural background with long-standing feelings of depression and multiple somatic complaints.

TECHNIQUE

Mann uses all the techniques of analytically oriented psychotherapy during the course of treatment, including dream and transference interpretations, although the latter are used mainly during the termination phase. These techniques are never used in a confronting manner nor are very deep interpretations given. Interpretations, when made, deal with the derivatives of conflicts and defenses and tend to follow the clinical material very closely. The tone of the treatment is one of support and encouragement. This supportive stance does not mean that the therapist has to give up his or her therapeutic neutrality, nor need details of the therapist's life be shared with the patient or other deviations be made from the traditional therapeutic role, except, of course, that the therapist is much more active in time-limited than in long-term therapy. Therapist activity is continually necessary to keep the treatment focused on the central issue. The frequent interventions of the therapist are also used to reinforce the production of meaningful material and the positive accomplishments of the patient. Through activity and empathy the therapist is able to convey to the patient that he or she is truly interested and also that the therapist is working as hard as the patient to accomplish the goals of the treatment. Mann emphasizes that encouragement should not be forced or "phony." Indeed, it is the sincere effort of working together in the therapy that contributes so much to the intense affect that is experienced throughout the treatment by both participants.

Mann also stresses the educational function of the therapist, that is, providing needed information which the patient has not acquired, either for psychological or cultural reasons. Education continues throughout the treatment and even beyond. Mann often tells his patients that transference feelings can be expected to occur after the termination of the actual treatment so that the patients are prepared to deal with and work through on their own some of the separation feelings that they will encounter in the posttreatment period.

The following fragment, from the fourth interview, is typical of Mann's style. When meeting what he believes to be strong defenses, he backs off and changes his interpretation to a more acceptable one.

DR: Has your husband ever said anything much about this business between you and your mother?

PT: No. He is getting more or less aggravated with the idea of me going out [to care for sick mother] every night. He thinks I should have more time to myself.

DR: When did he begin to think this way?

PT: This week, when I went out every night except Tuesday. He thought that was too much. She goes for her check-up, and if she's alright, I'll stop going down.

DR: Has he ever spoken before about this business of people asking you to do all the time?

PT: Yeah. He will always say, "Why can't you say no?" I never have an answer.

DR: Well, you have one answer. You are always afraid that if you say no, the other person will get hurt.

PT: The feeling that I have hurt somebody. I don't like to hurt anybody. Some people don't care what they say or do—as long as they do what they want, they don't care who is affected by it. But I can't be like that. (Although her fear that if she says no someone will be hurt clearly points up the extent of her unconscious rage, she is much too defended to allow for any kind of adequate exploration of this side of her feelings. In turn, the vigor of her defense dictates caution in the face of feelings that are intensely intolerable to her. I turn, therefore, to another more acceptable mode of examining her concern in respect to her own hostility.)

DR: Isn't there another way of looking at that? It's true, you know, that to hurt people for the hell of it is not a very nice thing, but if you are the kind of person who thinks that if you say no this will hurt the other person, might it not be that you are the kind of person who is afraid that she won't be liked?

PT: It could be.

DR: Do you think that you are the kind of person who has a special need to be liked?

PT: Maybe. I like to be wanted. I like to be accepted in groups or whoever is around. I wouldn't want to be shunned. (Mann 1973, p. 122)

FOLLOW-UP

Mann has conducted follow-up interviews with some of his patients 6 to 12 months after termination. While providing no systematic data, he reports that the results are generally good. The central issue is remembered clearly. The three phases of the treatment are recapitulated during the follow-up interview starting with feelings of optimism and reunion, followed by ambivalence and finally by a return of separation feelings. Mann feels that as a result of the treatment the patient has a more conscious awareness of earlier important events in his or her life with a resultant greater awareness of his or her affects and feelings about himself or herself and others. This in turn results in a greater tolerance for unpleasant affects and less reliance on automatic defense mechanisms in the future (Mann and Goldman 1982).

COUNTERTRANSFERENCE PROBLEMS

While this technique is relatively simple, it is not without problems for the therapist. The most important and almost universal countertransference problem is the tendency of the therapist to avoid dealing with the issue of separation and termination. As was noted above, this method exquisitely arouses in everyone, patient and therapist alike, the wish for timelessness, omnipotence, and immortality; so it is quite easy for the therapist to forget about the end of the treatment. The therapist, like the patient, may need reminders about how many treatment sessions are left. A useful technique is to head each session's process notes with the number of the session as well as with its date. From at least the ninth session onward the therapist's attention should be focused on looking for material that relates to the termination, and, as has been noted, if termination has not been brought up by the tenth session, the therapist should do so on his or her own.

The tendency of any therapist to drift away from the focus or central issue to follow leads which appear to be interesting is particularly troublesome when doing time-limited psychotherapy because deviations from the central issue into other areas are experienced by the patient as a tacit acknowl-edgment that the treatment indeed will be timeless and that all issues will be resolved. If the therapist strays from the central issue, the disillusionment necessary for the return to the reality of the second phase of the treatment will not occur. When termination occurs without the development of the second phase, the patient will experience the end of treatment as a major betrayal. To ask someone to go from feelings of omni-potence to nothing without adequate preparation is certainly not therapeutic.

Other difficulties can arise if the therapist does not be-lieve that anything meaningful can be accomplished in such a short period of treatment time. These doubts are usually stirred up when the patients ask, as they frequently do, if further treatment will be available if needed after the 12 sessions are completed. A vague answer from the therapist, such as "we'll see," means to the patient that the treatment will not *really* end and that he or she will therefore be able to avoid dealing with the issues of termination in a real and meaningful way. The therapist's attitude throughout the treatment must be that no further treatment will be needed. Doubts concerning the efficacy of the treatment can lead to other problems. As was discussed previously, the belief of the therapist is necessary for the development of the patient's feelings of omnipotence, which are an essential part of the first phase of the treatment. Also, if the therapist has doubts about the treatment, he or she may shy away from appropriate interpretations because of fears of uncovering too much material for the time available.

Difficulties will also occur if the therapist gives interpretations that are too deep. Because patients are not selected for this technique on the basis of psychological mindedness or self-awareness, care must be taken not to injure them with material with which they will not be able to deal. Deep interpretations are rarely appropriate in this technique.

TEACHING TIME-LIMITED PSYCHOTHERAPY

This technique is the easiest method of brief therapy to teach. The fixed number of sessions eliminates the need to decide when to terminate the treatment. The three phases of the treatment will develop because of the time limit; so the therapist will have an opportunity to observe these phenomena while still quite inexperienced in the technique. Furthermore, the level at which the therapy is conducted is similar to the beginnings of many long forms of therapy; so this technique does not present as radical a change for the therapist as do some of the other techniques. Of course, this method requires the acquisition of new skills, especially the determination and formulation of the central issue, and this does take time. As with all psychotherapy, it is best taught through individual supervision after the basic tenets have been learned.

SUMMARY

Time-limited psychotherapy is a brief psychotherapy technique of wide application. Only those with psychosis, severe depression, or borderline states are definitely excluded. There is a fixed time limit of 12 sessions which shapes the treatment into an opening phase characterized by the amelioration of symptoms and the production of much clinical material, a middle phase characterized by ambivalence, and a final phase characterized by the patient's experiencing and dealing with the separation from the therapist. The focus, here called the central issue, is framed in terms of long-standing, conscious feelings of distress. The attitude of the therapist is supportive and nonthreatening. The therapy is conducted on a level at which the derivatives of conflicts are dealt with rather than attempting to uncover the original core conflicts. The chief countertransference problems come from the therapist's avoidance of separation issues. Because of the set time limit and the use of the usual psychotherapy techniques, this is a relatively easy method to learn.

6

THE INTENSIVE BRIEF
PSYCHOTHERAPY
OF MALAN

In the years following World War II, Michael Balint, working in England, became interested in bringing the benefits of psychoanalytic psychology to those people who were unable to enter either a formal psychoanalysis or long-term psychoanalytic therapy. Balint's interest led to two major studies, one on the training of general practitioners in techniques of superficial psychotherapy (Balint 1957) and the other on the training of experienced analytically oriented psychotherapists in techniques of brief psychotherapy. David Malan worked with Balint on this latter project at the Tavistock Clinic in London and continued and expanded the work after Balint's death.

The work described in this chapter grew out of a workshop started by Balint in 1955. A group of experienced therapists met regularly and began to treat patients with brief therapy. As little was known about how to do this in a systematic way, the group had to develop its own selection criteria and techniques. At first they looked for relatively healthy patients with acute problems whom they hoped to treat with relatively superficial techniques. They soon found that there were not enough patients of this kind available, and they therefore started seeing people who were sicker than those whom they originally wanted to treat. Also, patients with recent acute onsets did not seem to come to the Tavistock Clinic, so that criterion was also dropped. Although the intention was to treat the patients with superficial techniques, the therapists soon noted that they were making deeper interpretations to their patients, in part because of their training, and in part because it became apparent that the patients could readily deal with the deeper interpretations. They noted that the patients responded well to the interpretations and that the therapy seemed to progress well. Out of these initial observations came *A Study of Brief Psychotherapy* (Malan 1963).

This book is a report of 21 patients treated with brief psychotherapy (10 to 40 sessions) and includes details of the patients and their treatments as well as follow-up studies on the patients after the termination of the treatment. Malan published two books on a second study of brief psychotherapy (Malan 1976a, 1976b). These books give a detailed account of the therapy of an additional 30 patients treated with brief psychotherapy and followed for a median of five and a half years after termination. Malan's clinical work grew out of his research experiences and was strongly influenced by the results of his research; so an understanding of the design and results of the research studies is a helpful introduction to Malan's system of brief psychotherapy. For the sake of simplicity, only the second study of brief psychotherapy will be considered here.

THE SECOND STUDY OF BRIEF PSYCHOTHERAPY

The basic design of the study was as follows. Selection criteria were established, and after a patient was interviewed and found acceptable for the study, independent raters studied the protocol and made specific predictions as to what would be considered a successful outcome. These predictions were based not only on symptomatic changes but also called for evidence of dynamic changes in the patient. Dynamic changes are those that result in the reorganization of the individual's defensive structure at a higher level of adaptation and functioning, in contrast to symptom removal or symptom substitution without such changes. The treatment would then proceed with a member of the study group. He or she would dictate detailed process notes on each interview, and the notes were later studied to determine the nature and quantity of the patient–therapist interactions. The protocol of the follow-up interview was studied by independent raters to determine how closely the predictions of success had been met. (Malan's book on the technical aspects of his study [1976b] will be of interest to anyone concerned with research on the outcome of any form of therapy.) Using very strict criteria for outcome, 9 patients were rated as having had successful brief therapy, 9 patients had unsuccessful brief therapy, 6 patients went on to successful long-term therapy, 2 patients had unsuccessful long-term therapy, and 4 patients were rated as "false" cases; that is, they showed improvement at follow-up, but it was thought to be due to external events and not due to the therapy. Only 1 patient out of the 30 studied was worse at follow-up.

The results of the study clearly demonstrated that important and apparently long-lasting symptomatic and dynamic changes could follow brief psychotherapy in patients with relatively extensive and long-lasting psychopathology. Correlations between content analysis and outcome showed strong positive correlations between interpretations linking the therapist with significant figures in the past (transference–parent [T–P] link) and good outcome. This statistic confirms not only that a deep interpretive approach is possible in brief treatments, but it also shows that the interpretations were most likely responsible for many of the good results that were seen. Further correlations showed that if a high degree of motivation and close adherence to a focus persisted from session five through session eight, the therapy would most likely end up a successful brief therapy. (A high motivation and low focality in sessions five to eight led to successful but long treatment, and low motivation and low focality in sessions five to eight led to unsuccessful brief therapy.)

SELECTION OF PATIENTS

Patients were selected for inclusion in the study of brief psychotherapy on the basis of a rather complicated procedure including some well-defined and other less clearly defined criteria. The study group met to consider possible patients and to evaluate the information presented in their referral forms. There were certain absolute contraindications which, if present, eliminated a patient from further consideration. These contraindications, adapted from the rejection criteria of the London Clinic for Psychoanalysis, excluded patients with a history of serious suicide attempts, drug addiction, convinced homosexuality, long-term hospitalization, more than one course of electroconvulsive therapy, chronic alcoholism, incapacitating chronic obsessional symptoms, incapacitating chronic phobic symptoms, and gross destructive or self-destructive acting out (Malan 1976a). If none of these exclusionary factors were present, the group would look for evidence of focality in the referral material, and if that was present, the patient was then seen for an initial interview.

During the initial interview, the evaluator would take a complete history to see if any of the above exclusionary factors could now be elicited. He or she would attempt to define the focus more clearly and, most importantly, would attempt a trial interpretation based on, if possible, a derivative of the proposed focus. A meaningful response to the trial interpretation became a condition for acceptance into the study. In addition, the ability to establish "contact" with the evaluator was a requirement. If the patient met these criteria, he or she was then given psychological tests consisting of the Rorschach and the Object Relations Test, in which the patient is required to tell a story about an ambiguous stimulus, similar to the Thematic Apperception Test (TAT).

After these data were collected patients were again presented to the study group, and if all the requirements were met, the group then tried to eliminate those for whom they predicted poor results in brief psychotherapy. This prediction was made on the basis of three factors. The first was the prediction that a patient would be unable to start effective work in the therapy in a brief period of time because of his or her inability to make contact, the necessity for prolonged work in order to generate sufficient motivation, or the presence of rigid defenses that would require a long time to penetrate. The second was the prediction that a patient would have difficulty terminating a brief treatment because of his or her "inevitable involvement in complex or deep-seated issues that there seems no hope of working through in a short time," a patient's severe dependence, or the probability of a patient's involvement in other deep transference formations (Malan 1976a, p. 69). The third factor leading to a prediction that the therapy would not exceed was based on the idea that in deep interpretative therapy there is a danger that the patient's previous depression or psychotic decompensation would be re-exacerbated, so that a patient with a history of serious depression or psychosis was eliminated. While these predictors of poor outcome would eliminate borderline or other severe character disorders, they do not result in the selection of only very healthy patients. As will be seen when the clinical material is presented later in this chapter, the selection criteria were broad enough to include a wide range of psychopathology.

SELECTION OF PATIENTS—CLINICAL CRITERIA

In his clinical work, Malan has directly adopted some of the selection criteria from the research studies. These include the need for a focus to be present and the necessity for the patient to respond to a trial interpretation. He also uses the exclusionary criteria of the London Clinic of Psychoanalysis mentioned above, and the same predictors of poor outcome that were outlined in the previous section are used to eliminate patients from brief treatment.

There is no time limit set on the initial evaluation, and it frequently requires one and a half to two hours. If more time is needed to get a thorough understanding of the patient, more time can be taken. While psychological tests are not used routinely, such tests are done if there is any question as to the presence of severe psychopathology or the level of the focus.

In addition to the complete psychiatric history, there is need for a complete psychodynamic history. By this is meant the accumulation of sufficient data to understand the patient's current symptomatology in relation to his or her earlier experiences and conflicts. The focus is determined on the basis of the psychodynamic history. The ideal focus is one where the current symptomatology and its precipitating stresses can be related to past occurrences of symptoms, and these in turn can be related to the original conflict in childhood. In the ideal case, this childhood conflict to which the focus is related is the nuclear conflict in the patient's mental organization. For Malan the conflict underlying the focus does not have to be, although it frequently is, oedipal in nature. He will treat people with preoedipal conflicts if the other criteria for selection are met.

The history also reveals the patient's capacity to form good relationships with people in his or her past and present environment. Past meaningful relationships, while not an absolute requirement, are a good indicator of the type of relationship that the patient will form in the therapy and are a guide to whether the patient will have difficulty in either starting or terminating the therapy. Difficulties in current relationships, such as a difficult marriage or living at home with parents in a complicated interaction, tend to lead to long treatments and may be a reason for not proceeding with a brief treatment plan.

The interaction with the evaluator is also, of course, an important consideration in selection. The idea of "contact" between examiner and patient means that the patient has the ability to relate to the examiner in a relatively brief period of time. The patient's attitudes about himself or herself are examined. If the patient has the capacity to speak honestly about himself or herself and to see his or her problems in psychological terms, it is a good prognostic sign. As noted above, great emphasis is placed on the trial interpretation and the patient's ability to respond to it.

Malan stresses not only the diagnostic value of the trial interpretation but also its therapeutic implications. A successful trial interpretation will tend to cement the patient–therapist relationship and start the therapeutic alliance because the patient will feel understood by the therapist, and, by producing new data or new feelings in his or her response to the interpretation, the patient will become actively involved in the treatment process. A well-motivated patient will appreciate the effect of the interpretation and will want to continue working with the therapist. This places a responsibility on the therapist if he or she decides not to treat the particular patient after the evaluation. Malan states that it is the responsibility of the therapist if he or she begins this type of evaluation with a patient to be prepared to make some sort of disposition that will be helpful to the patient. If the therapist knows that treatment facilities are not available, trial interpretations are best avoided. (Of course, if the patient does not respond to the trial interpretation, these particular problems will not arise.)

A corollary of this is that trial interpretations should be kept at the most superficial level necessary to elicit a response until the treatment contract has been definitely established. Trial interpretations should not be made until after the completion of the psychiatric history to make sure that there is no vulnerability to psychotic decompensation. A cogent interpretation in a vulnerable individual can precipitate an acute psychotic process.

An additional function of the trial interpretation is the testing of the focus. If there is no positive response, it may be that an incorrect focus has been chosen, and, after a reformulation by the therapist, another trial interpretation may be given. If the material warrants it, trial interpretations may take the form of transference interpretations.

The question of motivation is somewhat vague in Malan's writings. In the results of the study there is some correlation between motivation and outcome but not a very striking one. The data are complicated by the fact that motivation was one of the original selection criteria but was not clearly defined as such, except that the necessity for prolonged work to generate motivation was an exclusionary criterion. In his clinical work Malan states that there is a need for *some* motivation, but that often motivation can be increased by the work of the therapist in the early sessions of the treatment. The data demonstrate that if motivation is not high by the fifth to eighth session, a successful therapy is unlikely. Certainly the prognosis is better if the motivation is high at the initial interview and remains high throughout.

THE BEGINNING OF TREATMENT

In the research studies on brief psychotherapy no time limit was set at the beginning of the treatment. The patients were told that they would be seen for a brief period of time, a matter of months, and the hope was that something could be accomplished in that interval. They were also told that, if further treatment was required, they would be transferred to long-term therapy. They were told that, if the therapy was brief and successful, they still might be able to come back to see the therapist from time to time if they wished. The data on the follow-up studies are based on patients who received this type of introduction to the therapy. For some time, however, Malan, in his own clinical work and in his teaching, has been working with a fixed time limit set at the beginning of the treatment. He recommends 20 sessions for the ordinary patient with a therapist experienced in brief psychotherapy, and 30 sessions for the ordinary patient with an inexperienced therapist. Thirty sessions are used for an experienced therapist when issues of dependency are expected to be prominent or when multiple foci are being worked with. The date of termination is set at the beginning of treatment. Despite the fixed time limit, the patient is told that he or she will be able to see the therapist after treatment ends on a regular basis if he or she wishes to. Malan, in contrast to Mann, believes that leaving this option open for the patient in no way diminishes the impact of the termination. The patient represses the possibility of further contact, and the termination is experienced as though it were final.

While the therapist has a firm idea of the focus that is to be worked with at the beginning of the treatment, the patient is usually not asked to agree explicitly to working on the focus, that is, no formal contract is set up. The focus may have been discussed with the patient in the course of the evaluation and, if possible, confirmed by a trial interpretation; so both patient and therapist usually have a clear picture of the issues to be worked on.

TECHNIQUE

The aim of the treatment is the clarification of the triangle of insight and the defense–anxiety–impulse triad. The triangle of insight involves the patient's awareness of his or her conflict as it is played out with the therapist (T), with other people in his or her current life (O), and with significant people, usually parents, in his or her past (P). In each of these areas it is possible to see the defenses the patient uses, the impulses that are being defended against, and the anxiety that the conflict mobilizes. While it is important to clarify all components of the triangles, what is most important in order to achieve insight and to alleviate symptoms is the clarification of the impulse component of the past conflict. As can be seen, this formulation is valid for all forms of analytically oriented insight therapy, including psychoanalysis, and is not by any means specific for brief therapy. Malan believes it is possible to achieve all these goals within the time limits set by his treatment, in properly selected patients using properly trained therapists.

The techniques used by Malan are identical to the techniques used in standard analytically oriented therapy. The defense–anxiety–impulse triad is generally approached by first interpreting the defenses, including, of course, resistances. Then, when the material warrants it, the impulse may be interpreted, usually with its accompanying anxiety. The area chosen for the work depends on the material. Usually it starts with persons in the current life (O) and then shifts to the transference. Sometimes the conflict is interpreted in the transference first. Usually the past conflict is interpreted after the other areas have been clarified. As has been noted above, data from the research studies confirm that the transference–parent interpretations (T–P links) are the most important factors in the successful therapy.

Dreams, fantasies, slips, and associations are utilized in the usual manner, although, because of time limitations, dreams and fantasies are not analyzed as fully as they would be in a long-term treatment. The question may be raised as to how it is possible to use all the standard techniques and end up with a brief therapy. Malan has said that if you start with a focal patient, the therapy is going to be a brief and focal one. In the ideal patient the therapist does not need to modify his or her technique at all except that he or she must follow the patient's lead and not digress into other areas of interest to the therapist. As the patient deviates from the ideal, the therapist must become more active to keep the therapy in focus. The activity consists of "selective interpretation, selective attention, and selective neglect" (Malan 1976a, p. 32). While working within the focus, the therapist need be neither unduly confronting, nor need he or she shrink from deep interpretations. If the material warrants it, transference–parent links can be made in relation to such issues as castration anxiety and sexual impulses.

While Malan stresses the importance of working deeply in brief therapy, he also indicates that it is not *always* necessary to do so to get good results. Indeed, some of the successful treatments in his research series showed no evidence of any transference interpretations or T–P links. What his work has shown is that it is possible to do deep, meaningful interpretive work in brief psychotherapy, so that no one should feel that brief psychotherapy is *limited* to superficial techniques.

(Malan has worked with multiple foci in a given patient, limited foci in sicker patients, as well as deeper therapy with most disturbed patients, but there is insufficient data available on these areas, and this work is beyond the scope of this book.)

In recent years, Malan has been moving toward the techniques of Davanloo and is changing some of the methods described in this chapter. This in no way diminishes the value of the work that he has done with his own techniques.

TERMINATION

In patients with an oedipal focus, termination is usually not an issue and does not become an important part of the treatment. On the other hand, in patients where preoedipal issues are central, separation and, therefore, termination are of critical importance and must be dealt with in the treatment. As with other issues, an attempt is made to deal with the termination in the transference and to make the appropriate transference–parent links. The last third of the treatment is generally used for dealing with termination issues in patients with a preoedipal focus.

In his research series Malan has presented a number of patients whose therapy continued uninterrupted after the 40-session upper limit of brief therapy had been reached, and subsequently ended as either successfully or unsuccessfully treated long-term cases. As there is no basic difference in technique between this short-term therapy and long-term therapy, the same therapist can continue the treatment with relatively little damage to the treatment or to the transference, particularly when no definite termination time has been set. (When a definite termination date has been set, the issues of the "failure" of the brief therapy must be dealt with.) Indeed, Malan feels that one of the main contributions of his research in brief therapy is to show the continuity between brief, medium-length, and long-term analytically oriented therapies and to show that the same mechanisms apply in all these situations.

PROBLEMS FOR THE THERAPIST

The chief problem in using this technique occurs because the technique is similar to longer forms of therapy. The therapist who is used to doing long-term analytically oriented psychotherapy may find himself or herself drifting into old patterns and analyzing anything that comes along without staying within the focus. This will lead to long-term and not brief therapy. Unless the patient is unusually well focused, the therapist must be constantly on guard lest therapeutic zeal and curiosity lead him or her astray.

Another danger for the beginning therapist in this technique lies in becoming overly ambitious and doing "wild" analysis, making deep interpretations for the sake of making deep interpretations even when the material does not warrant it. As Malan has noted, when this therapy is done well, the same uncovering and unfolding is seen as occurs in long-term therapy. An interpretation, when correct, will be followed by the production of new material or the release of heretofore blocked affect. When the confirmation is not forthcoming, the therapist must reassess the situation, either interpreting the resistance or checking to make sure that his or her formulation is the correct one.

FOLLOW-UP STUDIES—CASE MATERIAL

Malan's follow-up studies are among the most elegant in the entire psychiatric literature. His method of predicting and evaluating both dynamic and symptomatic improvement is one that can be applied to any form of psychotherapy. (Malan has studied group therapy patients and untreated patients using the same techniques.) Because his work is the most notable demonstration to date of what can be accomplished with brief psychotherapy, a few of his successful cases will be presented in some detail.

The following are summaries of seven cases rated as successful on follow-up in Malan's second series of brief psychotherapies (1976a). It is difficult to generalize about the techniques used in these treatments as they were done by different therapists at a time when the techniques of brief psychotherapy were being developed and had not yet been formalized. In addition, no extensive verbatim transcripts of the actual treatments are given, so that it is not possible to get a detailed picture of what actually went on in the sessions. However, extensive information about the presenting problems, history, general course of treatment, and follow-up data is given for each patient in the entire series. The patients are identified by the pseudonyms used by Malan, so that the reader can refer to the original case material for more details. What is particularly striking is that most of the patients showed improvement in long-standing characterological disturbances as well as symptom removal. This is, of course, not coincidental, as Malan's criteria for success include this kind of overall change in functioning.

The Almoner (social worker)

This 22-year-old single woman came for treatment because of a few months history of difficulty remembering things at her work, difficulty in making decisions regarding her career, and feelings of depression and poor self-esteem. The evaluator felt that the patient used a general defense of keeping everything "nice" and had great difficulty expressing any kind of anger, especially toward her parents.

During the early part of the treatment the patient began to experience some of her feelings of anger at her parents. She was able to move to a better job. When in session seven the therapist told the patient of his forthcoming vacation, the patient said she thought she had benefited enough and could end the treatment. The therapist disagreed. During the therapist's vacation, the patient had had her first open quarrel with her parents and temporarily broke relations with them, about which the patient felt good. Upon the therapist's return the patient was able to attack him somewhat and then insisted on ending treatment despite the therapist's recommendation. She wrote him a letter saying that she felt like a completely different person as a result of the therapy.

Follow-up interviews at 6 months, 13 months, and 5 years 8 months revealed the following. The patient had had a rapid reconciliation with her parents and reestablished an ongoing relationship with them at a much better level than previously. She was married, had two children, and was functioning well. She was able to be open about her feelings with her husband, although perhaps she did not assert herself quite as strongly as she might have, and she no longer needed to keep things nice. She was more at ease socially than before treatment.

The Buyer

This 27-year-old man came for treatment after a one-and-a-half-hour "blackout" which occurred after his fiancée had broken their recent engagement because of the opposition of her father. He had had a similar blackout while in the military when an officer whom he disliked gave him too much responsibility. The evaluator also felt that the patient was generally not as effective as he might be and that he caused people to dislike him by his manner of false overpoliteness.

Initially, there was poor motivation, which the therapist confronted directly. Motivation increased after session 5, and the patient became more aware of his repressed sexual and aggressive impulses. In session 11 the patient's murderous feelings were openly acknowledged by the patient and were linked to the oedipal triangle. The therapy was scheduled to end after 16 sessions, but at that time the patient was once again trying to resolve the situation with his fiancée, so that the treatment was extended by two sessions. Termination issues were not really dealt with.

On follow-ups at one year seven months and seven years three months, there were no additional blackouts. He had married another woman and had a satisfactory relationship with her, albeit there was a low interest in sex on his part. His facade of false politeness was gone. He was able to be much more effective in his work and with men in general, and he had successfully started and maintained his own business.

The Gibson Girl

This 18-year-old single saleswoman came for treatment because of incapacitating fears of fainting when in crowds. The evaluator felt the patient related in a superficial manner during the evaluation and with people in her life in general.

In session 4 the patient revealed for the first time that her father was an alcoholic, and this was followed by increasing criticism of both parents. After an interpretation in session 10 that the fear of fainting was related to the primal scene, the patient began going out by herself in a limited way. In session 22 the patient's wish to have sex with her boyfriend began to be interpreted, followed by the patient's acknowledgment of her ignorance of sexual matters and the revelation that the symptoms started right after the boyfriend began to press her about having sex. At the next session the patient reported she had gotten a job and wanted to end therapy, which she gradually did, despite the therapist wanting the patient to work more on her sadistic impulses. There were a total of 28 sessions.

On follow-up after five years eight months, the patient had no phobias except that she did not ride the subway. She married the original boyfriend and had a good marriage and was able to enjoy sex. There was evidence for a deepening of relations with both husband and children. There was still some difficulty with her parents, the father having been overidealized and the mother a source of ongoing anger, although the conflict was of minor proportions in the patient's life.

The Indian Scientist

This 29-year-old man came for treatment because of premature ejaculation of six years duration. Although this was only a problem in selected situations, it became evident in the evaluation that the patient had difficulty being successful in his studies and in his career. He had difficulties with people in authority. During the evaluation interview, the therapist interpreted to the patient his fear and guilt about fighting with his successful and aggressive father and his tendency to give in when he was beaten in a fight.

The therapy focused on the patient's equating achievement with taking his father's sexual powers, which was followed by new material concerning the patient's love for his mother and jealousy of his father. There were few transference interpretations given, although the patient changed his attitude about the therapist being authoritarian during the course of the therapy. The total treatment was 12 sessions spread over a one-year period.

On follow-up seven years four months later (by letter as the patient was out of the country), the patient stated he was happily married and had no sexual problems. He was successful in his career and enjoyed the work he was doing.

Mrs. Morley

This 60-year-old widow came to treatment wanting to improve her relationship with her daughter. She tended to be overintrusive and tactless in her relations with her children, which led to many disagreements. Psychological tests showed that the patient tended to ward off depression by "absorbing" people into herself.

The therapy proceeded on a superficial level, helping the patient to recognize her contributions to the tension between herself and her daughter. There were five weekly sessions and four other sessions at irregular intervals over a five-month period.

On follow-up after five years four months the patient was able to tolerate loneliness, had her own interests and activities, and was able to maintain good relations with her children, although there was some strain involved. There was some depression, although no major depressive episodes had occurred.

The Pesticide Chemist

This 31-year-old married man, always a perfectionist, came for treatment after he lost control of his anger, hit his wife, and cried for three hours thereafter. In the previous six months he had been bothered by criticism from his boss, felt a general lack of energy, and his chronic problem of premature ejaculation became worse.

The therapy was an interpretive one. The therapist led up to the triangle of insight by showing the patient that his overconscientiousness was an attempt to control his rage at his father for not loving him enough, and that, when he was criticized for this effort by his wife, his boss, and by the therapist, the patient lost control. This was followed by the patient's recognizing that he could not satisfy everybody and revealing that he saw his wife as sexually demanding while doing little for him. After this he was more assertive with his wife about her lack of sexual interest, but when she responded to this approach, he became somewhat ambivalent about the treatment and ended it without any termination work after 14 sessions. Two months later there was improvement at work, the patient being able to stand up to the boss, as well as at home where there was greater sexual compatibility.

Follow-ups at one year two months and three years ten months revealed progress at work where the patient was able to handle greater responsibilities and deal effectively with authority. Indeed, he was able to develop new techniques for coping with his boss during the follow-up period. However, there were increased marital difficulties, in part resulting from an "emotional crisis" in the wife which resulted in diminished sexual activity.

The Zoologist

This 22-year-old single man presented with the following complaints: a two-year history of inability to concentrate on his school work, a 14-month history of severe indigestion with negative medical work-up, and an 8-month history of depression including suicidal ideation. He had dropped out of school 5 months previously and, at the time of seeking treatment, wanted to return to his studies. In addition to these complaints, the evaluator noted much repressed anger against his parents, who wanted him to pursue a profession, and difficulty experiencing closeness with women. The major part of the initial interview was characterized by lack of affect and spontaneity, but this changed when the interviewer, who continued as the therapist, interpreted the patient's difficulty in expressing feelings. This led to a discussion of the patient's need to get closer to people.

The treatment was originally scheduled for 16 sessions, but it actually continued at irregular intervals for three years. The therapy was delayed by the vacation of the therapist, and, when it did begin, the patient was again well defended. In session 4 the patient spoke of the barriers he put up against people, and the therapist made an interpretation in which he linked the barriers to defenses against anger at being unloved by parents, people in his current life, and the therapist. In session 9 the patient became angry with the therapist because his relations on the outside were getting worse. The therapist interpreted his pattern of spoiling things people had given him when he was angry with them, linking his spoiling his college career as an expression of anger at his parents to his spoiling his outside relationships at that time as an expression of anger at the therapist. This was followed by emotional relief and an admission that he had quit school to spite his father. As the result of a dream in session 16, anger at termination was dealt with, leading to an acknowledgment of warmth and love for the therapist in the next session. After this stage of the treatment the patient returned to school and began dating women. When there was difficulty with a woman, he became depressed and returned for some additional sessions. He eventually became engaged but found an old diary of his fiancée's telling of other men, after which he became more severely depressed. The patient returned one year later to say that his wife was now cold to him. The therapist reinterpreted the original conflict, now in terms of the wife and the therapist: that he was angry with and disappointed in the wife, expressed it by spoiling the relationship, and that the wife was really just reacting to his behavior. Similarly, he might be spoiling his life in order to express his anger at the therapist. The patient then showed much emotion and admitted that he had indeed precipitated the distance in the marriage. There was a total of 32 sessions in a three-and-a-half-year period.

Follow-up was three and a half years after termination and seven years after the start of the therapy. At this time the patient was still married and had children. He felt that his marriage was good and that there were no sexual problems, but the evaluator felt there was some distance in the relationship and that he handled conflict by avoidance. On the other hand, his professional life was in good order, he was happy with his work and successful at it. There was one recurrence of gastric symptoms when he was working with a difficult man. He resolved the situation by getting a job where he could work more independently, and there has been no recurrence since. There was no recurrence of depression.

SUMMARY

Malan has developed a technique of brief psychotherapy using the standard techniques of psychoanalytically oriented psychotherapy, that is, the interpretation of defenses, leading to the interpretation of the nuclear conflict and its accompanying anxiety in the transference, as well as in the patient's current life and in his or her past. Patients with either an oedpial or a preoedipal focus may be suitable. When a preoedipal focus is selected, termination issues are dealt with. Selection is based on the presence of a focus, evidence of the patient's response to trial interpretations during the initial interview, and the presence of at least some motivation for change. Patients are excluded if they meet certain criteria indicating previous serious psychopathology or if it is felt brief psychotherapy would not be successful because the patient would be difficult to engage in treatment, would be difficult to terminate, or if there is evidence for possible serious decompensation during the course of the therapy. A time limit of 20 to 30 sessions is set at the start of the treatment. Malan has done research utilizing these techniques which indicates that far-ranging changes can occur and can be maintained over a prolonged follow-up period. His studies indicate that interpreting the link between the transference and similar feelings and attitudes toward significant persons in the patient's past is highly correlated with successful outcomes. Because these techniques are so similar to ordinary long-term therapy, care must be taken by the therapist lest he or she drift into the usual patterns of dealing with whatever material is presented by the patient rather than staying within the focus. If careful attention is not paid to maintaining the focus, the therapy will turn into a long-term treatment.

7

THE BROAD-FOCUS SHORT-TERM DYNAMIC PSYCHOTHERAPY OF DAVANLOO

Davanloo began his work on brief psychotherapy in 1962 at the Montreal General Hospital. Like the other workers in the field, he developed the main components of his technique independently and did not become aware of what Sifneos and Malan were doing until his own work was well established. As early as 1963 Davanloo began a formal research project. Between 1963 and 1974 he evaluated 575 patients of whom 23 percent (130) were found suitable for his brief therapy. Of the 130 treated, 115 were thought to have been treated successfully. The treated patients were seen for an average of 20 sessions. Follow-up data were obtained on 40 percent of the treated patients, the follow-up period ranging from two to seven years. It was found that the gains that the patients had demonstrated at the end of the therapy were maintained throughout the follow-up period.

Davanloo's technique is applicable to a variety of patients, including not only those with an oedipal focus or a focus involving specific losses but also some patients suffering from long-standing neurotic and characterological problems involving more than one focus. Unfortunately, Davanloo has not published his work in a detailed and systematic manner. While he has published numerous verbatim excerpts showing his technique with patients (Davanloo 1978, 1979, 1980), he has published no extensive case studies of his treatments. In particular, the details of his work with the sicker patients, where his most unique contribution lies, have not yet been published. What follows is an attempt at systematization, based on the published material, with the addition of material obtained at workshops where Davanloo spoke about his technique.

SELECTION OF PATIENTS

Davanloo stresses the evalution interviews. From the very outset of the evaluation process, the therapist engages in a trial therapy; that is, the major techniques which characterize this method of treatment are employed by the therapist from his or her first contact with the patient. The purpose is not only to determine whether the patient is suitable for this type of therapy, but also, by making therapeutic interventions from the beginning, to start the treatment process during the evaluation interviews, resulting in the formation of an early therapeutic alliance and the production of much material during the initial interviews. Because the evaluation process and the treatment process are similar, it is difficult to understand how the evaluation is done until one also understands how the treatment is conducted.

In addition to conducting the trial therapy, the evaluator must gather enough data to make a clinical, dynamic, and genetic diagnosis. He or she must also evaluate the following ego functions of the patient which Davanloo (1978) considers important in the selection process.

Quality of Human Relationships. Here the evaluator is most interested in the type of relationship that the patient forms with the evaluator. The ability to form a good relationship in the clinical situation correlates well, of course, with the ability to form good relationships in other areas of the patient's life. Care must be taken to separate those difficulties in interaction which are caused by the patient's symptoms, such as depression, from those difficulties in interaction that are a result of a more basic defect in the patient. Because the patient's symptoms can interfere with his or her ability to relate during the interview, the evaluator is also interested in obtaining a good history of relationships which the patient has had with significant people in the past as well as in his or her current life. The evaluator looks for "give and take" relationships rather than exploitative ones. Particular attention is paid to the history of sexual relationships, as Davanloo has found that a history of promiscuous sexual relationships often results in longer and less satisfactory treatments.

The Affective Function of the Ego.   This is of great importance to Davanloo. As will be seen below when Davanloo's technique is described, he places much more emphasis on mobilizing specific affects in the course of the treatment than do other workers in the field. It is, therefore, not surprising that the patient's ability to demonstrate affect in the evaluation is stressed. During the course of the evaluation, the evaluator attempts whenever possible to mobilize the patient's affect in order to see not only whether the patient is capable of experiencing and feeling the affect, but also whether the patient is able to tolerate the affect once it has been mobilized. Thus, for example, when the patient demonstrates anxiety as a result of probing questions from the evaluator, the evaluator observes whether this anxiety is handled in such a way as to lead to new material or a positive shift in the defensive structure, or to an immobilization of the patient, regressive defenses, or breakdowns in the thinking process. Similarly, with other affects such as guilt, depression, and anger it is important to note not only whether the patient has a flexible and full range of affect but also whether experiencing the affect is well tolerated. The inability to tolerate strong affect or the development of regressive symptoms as a result of the mobilization of the affect is a contraindication for this form of treatment. On the other hand, when the affect is either directly experienced or is close to the surface and can be mobilized relatively easily during the course of the evaluation interview, and the affect is well tolerated by the patient, it is an indication that the patient will probably do well in the treatment. During the evaluation, the evaluator takes every opportunity to mobilize affect that is latent until satisfied that he or she understands the affective functioning of the patient.

Motivation. Davanloo rates the patient on degree of motivation for change. The goals of the patient are assessed to determine whether or not they are realistic. In addition, the patient's motivation for treatment is clarified. Those patients who are looking only for a regressive experience in the treatment are not selected. Davanloo has found that during the course of the evaluation process the patient's motivation will often increase in response to interpretations by the therapist; therefore, motivation should be assessed throughout the course of the evaluation, not just at the beginning of the interviews. It is a good prognostic sign if there is an increase in motivation in response to an interpretation.

Psychological Mindedness. Here the patient's capacity and motivation for introspection and his or her ability to communicate thoughts, feelings, and fantasies are evaluated. The patient's ability to see how intrapsychic productions are related to past experiences is determined. True psychological mindedness is differentiated from obsessive rumination and intellectualization.

Response to Interpretation. This is one of the most important selection criteria for Davanloo. He looks not only for a cognitive response to an interpretation but also for an affectual response. A full response to a transference interpretation is particularly significant. As has been noted, the same confronting technique is used during the evaluation interview as will be used throughout the therapy. Therefore, if the patient responds to this technique during the evaluation it is likely he or she will continue to respond to it during the therapy. (It may sound simple to say that those patients who respond well to a technique will respond well to that technique, yet it is surprising how few therapists actually use this method of selection.)

Intelligence. The patient needs to be of above-average intelligence in order to be able to deal with the intellectual concepts that are a part of the treatment. Davanloo does not give specific criteria for evaluating intelligence. Here again, as in other areas of the evaluation, it is important to separate those inhibitions of intelligence caused by symptoms or interactions with the evaluator from the deficiencies due to the patient's basic endowment.

The Ego's Defensive Psychological Organization.   Here the primary defenses of the patient are evaluated. If therapy is to be successful, the defenses must be flexible. The flexibility of the defenses is evaluated throughout the course of the evaluation interviews. As the defenses of the patient are challenged by the evaluator, the shifts in the patient's defensive functioning can be studied. The predominant and rigid use of primitive defenses is a contraindication for this type of treatment, although if a primitive defense appears only transiently, it is not a contraindication. Patients are rejected when the predominant defenses are "intense reliance on projection, massive denial, major reliance on acting out in dealing with conflicts, acting out combined with projection, or a few rigid persistently used ego defense mechanisms" (Davanloo 1978, p. 19).

In addition to the ego functions listed above, the transference reactions of the patient are evaluated throughout the initial interviews. The patient comes to the initial interview with preexisting ideas, expectations, and fantasies, both conscious and unconscious, about the therapist. Evidence of this preexisting and characteristic transference pattern can be seen during the interview. In response to specific attributes of the therapist, and especially in response to the interventions that the therapist will make during the evaluation, more specific transference reactions will emerge as well. The therapist needs to respond rapidly to these varied transference manifestations. It is an important part of the evaluation process to obtain as complete and accurate a picture of the patient's transference manifestations as possible. If the patient forms a transference too readily, this might be a contraindication to treatment, suggesting a borderline personality structure. The therapist should also be aware of any countertransference difficulties that he or she may have with this particular patient lest they interfere with the evaluation and the treatment. If the therapist has doubts about this, an evaluation with a different therapist is indicated.

At the conclusion of the evaluation process, which may take up to three hours in separate interviews, the patient and the therapist agree on the focus for the treatment. The ther-

apist presents as full a formulation of the presenting problem as
is possible, including links to the transference, the current life
situation, and the significant past figures of the patient. In
addition, the patient is informed of the approximate length of
the treatment. No definite time limit is set.

Davanloo has found that if the patient is highly motivated
and very responsive to the trial therapy and there is a simple
oedpial focus, the therapy will take from 5 to 10 sessions. If
the patient is highly motivated and very responsive and there
is a single focus, but the focus involves loss, the treatment will
last from 5 to 15 sessions. This group of highly motivated,
single-focus patients comprises only 2 percent of those seeking therapy at the Montreal General Hospital. The remaining
patients selected for brief therapy comprise 33 percent of
those seeking treatment; these patients are treated in 15 to 40
sessions, the exact number depending on the complexity of the
pathology, the degree of resistance shown, and the experience
of the therapist. If the patients meet the selection criteria,
diagnosis or chronicity is not a determinant of treatability.
Thus Davanloo has treated people with multiple foci and
longstanding severe psychopathology. His technique is particularly useful for patients with long-standing obsessive or
phobic symptoms.

TECHNIQUE

THE OPENING PHASE

Treatment is conducted through weekly, face-to-face sessions. The patient is asked to talk about whatever comes to
mind. The therapist maintains neutrality—he or she does not
give direct advice, does not answer personal questions or talk
about himself or herself, and does not engage in conversations
with the patient outside of the sessions. Despite the therapist's
vigorous confrontations of the patient, he or she remains calm.

The major contribution which Davanloo has made to the
technique of brief psychotherapy is his gentle but relentless
confrontation of the patient, particularly confrontations designed to enable the patient to consciously experience anger.
During the opening phase of the treatment, which usually
comprises the first five sessions, the therapist concentrates on

the patient's feelings, especially feelings about the therapist. The main technique used is the repeated questioning of the patient, asking what he or she feels at that particular moment. The skill and sensitivity of the therapist enable him or her to pick up on minimal cues from the patient such as pauses, minor changes in affect, subtle shifts in content, or changes in body movements, which indicate some resistance to the therapist. It is important for the therapist to pick up on even the most minor evidence of resistance as soon as possible. When these signs are brought to the patient's attention, and the affect can be surfaced, there is a relief of tension and an increase in the patient's motivation. If these manifestations of resistance are permitted to pass unchallenged, the resistance will grow, the motivation will decrease, there will be an impairment of the therapeutic alliance, and the therapy will not progress. When the patient is challenged as to what he or she is feeling at a particular moment, often he or she will give vague, evasive, and qualified responses. The therapist, again relentlessly, does not permit the patient to remain vague and evasive and challenges the patient to be more specific as to the exact feelings at that particular moment. Qualifying words and phrases such as "probably," "I guess," "I suppose," and "perhaps" are challenged until the patient is able to acknowledge his or her thoughts and feelings, specifically and accurately without qualification. The process during this phase of the therapy tends to be a circular one. The therapist's probing questions anger the patient. The patient mobilizes defenses against the conscious awareness and expression of the anger. These defenses usually take the form of increased passivity and the type of evasiveness mentioned above. The therapist then intensifies the patient's anger by challenging these defenses. Eventually the patient is able to express the anger openly in the treatment situation. The fact that the patient is able to feel and express the anger without any bad consequences either to himself or herself or to the therapist serves as a reassuring and desensitizing experience for the patient. The surfacing and accepting of the anger serves to further the therapeutic alliance and increases the motivation that the patient has for the treatment.

The tone that Davanloo employs during the opening phase of the treatment, and continues throughout the entire treatment, is one of gentle firmness. He does not engage in the type of provocative challenging of the patient that Sifneos does. Davanloo presents himself to the patient as strong, serious, calm, self-assured, and somewhat authoritarian, but at the same time he conveys his capacity for empathy and concern.

In addition to confronting and challenging the patient, Davanloo is also supportive. There is great emphasis on giving the patient the major responsibility for the treatment and making him or her feel an equal of the therapist. The therapist frequently asks whether the patient agrees with what is being said. With such phrases as "have you noticed how you do this?" and "of course, it's up to you," the therapist encourages the patient to be an active participant in the treatment. There are frequent recapitulations of the major issues uncovered during the treatment, both by the therapist and by the patient in response to the therapist's request. In addition, the therapist often acknowledges the patient's suffering. Davanloo usually shakes hands with patients at the end of the session. These supportive techniques are a necessary counterbalance to the authoritarian confrontations. If the balance is not kept, the patient may experience the therapy as an assault or a humiliation.

As the feelings and the defenses against the feelings become evident in the treatment situation, they are pointed out to the patient. Attempts are then made to uncover similar feelings and defenses in relation to significant people in the patient's current life and then to show similar feelings and defenses in relation to significant people in the patient's past. As can be seen, what Davanloo does here is to interpret the triangle of insight as soon as possible in terms of the transference (T), the significant people in the patient's current life (C), and the significant people in the patient's past life (P). Similarly, the impulse, the defense against the impulse, and the anxiety raised by the impulse are interpreted as soon as possible in all three areas. These are the same TCP interpretations which figure prominently in Malan's work (Chapter 6). Davanloo, like Malan, has found correlations between TCP interpretations and successful therapy. He has found that the earlier TCP interpretations can be made, the shorter the therapy will tend to be.

In elucidating the details of the patient's feelings and reactions to people in his or her current life and in his or her past, relentless questioning is again the primary technique, the aim here being to have the patient be as *specific* as possible about the actual details of his or her current life and past experiences. Just as it is important for the patient to be specific about his or her feelings, so too is it important for the patient to be specific about the actual events of his or her life. This technique does not permit the patient to evade issues by means of vagueness and generalities. As the patient produces more material, the therapist can use this material, together with the dynamic formulations that he or she has made, to respond with "subtly loaded words" in order to speak directly to the patient's unconscious (Davanloo 1980, p. 63). Thus, when it was hypothesized that castration anxiety played an important part in a patient's conflict, the therapist introduced the phrase that the patient was afraid of being "cut off" to refer to the patient's fear of people in authority. This use of emotionally charged words, similar to Felix Deutsch's technique of the associative anamnesis, serves to heighten the patient's feeling of being understood by the therapist and, therefore, heighten the therapeutic alliance.

During the first phase of therapy, there is a lessening of tension and some production of new material, but this is quickly followed by an increase in resistance so that the process of challenging the patient's resistance, getting the patient to acknowledge feelings of anger toward the therapist, and pointing out the patient's characteristic defenses against the anger is repeated over and over. It is only after multiple repetitions of the above process that the resistance "melts away" and the outpouring of material characteristic of the midphase of the treatment occurs.

Davanloo uses his technique of treatment during the evaluation interview as a trial therapy in order to see who can benefit from his technique. Thus, very early in the evaluation interview, the evaluator attempts to confront the patient with his or her feelings in the transference, specifically with feelings of anger toward the therapist and with his or her characteristic defenses against the anger. Just as in the opening phase of therapy, where the interpretation of the transference anger leads to a heightened motivation, a heightened therapeutic alliance, and a flow of significant material, so too during the initial interview, if the transference is interpreted first, the history-taking process will be enhanced and significant material will be uncovered which ordinarily might not be available to the evaluator. It can be seen, therefore, that confrontation of the patient about his or her feelings toward the therapist should occur early in the course of the evaluation.

Here are some examples of Davanloo's techniques during evaluation interviews. The same technique is used during the opening phase of the treatment. The first fragment shows Davanloo confronting the patient's defenses and elucidating the patient's subsequent anger at the therapist. The therapist then links the patient's feelings toward the therapist with his past feelings toward his mother (the T–P link).

TH: Then your relationship with your mother has become much worse since your father left?

PT: Yes, because in a sense I've realized certain things about her.

TH: What are the things you've realized about her?

PT: Let's say it came to a point where this hate of her still keeping him in the house, which I still feel for her—I felt that hate even after he had left because I felt it was too late, let's say. Look, you're affected after a certain many years. Could you repeat your question?

TH: What do you think happened that you forgot my question?

PT: What do you mean?

TH: I was wondering what happened. Do you usually forget?

PT: No.

TH: What do you think happened here?

PT: I don't know. I was just thinking of something and all of a sudden it blanked out.

TH: Does it usually happen that way to you?

PT: No, not usually.

TH: How do you feel about me questioning you?

PT: I feel you're very aggressive with your questions.

TH: And how do you feel?

PT: A little bit on edge.

TH: Do you feel irritated?

PT: Yes.

TH: Do you think the forgetfulness had to do with that?

PT: In what respect do you mean?

TH: Because, in a way, what you are saying is this: that I was in a way repeatedly facing you with the problem, and you have a tendency to run away from the problem. Do you see what I mean?

PT: I know.

TH: Obviously, here I am confronting you with certain issues, and insisting that you look at them, and I didn't let you run away from them. Then you got irritated. Okay?

PT: Yes.

TH: Now, let's look at your irritation. What was it that you were experiencing inside?

PT: I just felt I was trying to explain something and it wasn't coming through to you, and you would pound on me with more questions.

TH: And that reminds you of what? Is there any other person with whom you have had an experience like this?

PT: Yes.

TH: Who?

PT: My mother.

TH: She pounds on you?

PT: Let's say there are certain times when I get aggravated at her, and I try to explain, and it's impossible because she's kind of out of touch with what's going on. She has her own problems; she's seeing a psychiatrist, and she'll avoid the questions and avoid my talking and switch from that automatically to something else, or start hurting me by saying certain things. So it's impossible to have any kind of argument with her on a rational basis. I can't, so that frustrates me more, and I hide myself in my room because I can't take it.

TH: So one thing that came out was that here with me you feel irritated; do you think your forgetfulness had to do with that?

PT: Maybe.

TH: Why do you say "maybe"? (Davanloo 1978, pp. 296–297)

The following three fragments are taken from a two-hour evaluation interview with a young woman. The first shows the therapist confronting the patient with her vagueness and then linking her reactions to the therapist with her reactions to her boyfriend and others in her current life (the T–C link). At the end of the fragment there is the affect-laden production of new confirmatory material.

TH: You said you are a contradictory person. How about right now here with me?

PT: Have I contradicted myself?

TH: What do you think?

PT: Well, yeah, I do contradict.

TH: You see, right now we are looking into your difficulties. You said that you have some difficulties and that you want to look at them.

PT: Yeah. I suppose . . .

TH: Why do you say "suppose"? Do you, or don't you?

PT: Well, I have difficulties, sure. I always say, "Well, it could be worse," you know. And it doesn't seem so bad.

TH: How do you feel about coming here and wanting to discuss your problems with me?

PT: With you?

TH: Uh-huh.

PT: I feel okay about it.

TH: Let's look at your relationship here with me. I have a feeling that on one hand you are here, and on the other hand you are not here. You have not been specific in what you have told me so far. Do you notice that you leave things hanging in the middle of nowhere?

PT: I am being evasive; I know that.

TH: And that is really the issue. Are you specific, or are you evasive? We are here to see what the problems are, your difficulties. But if you say there is, and at the same time you say there isn't and continue to be vague and evasive, then we won't be able to understand the problem, and we will not have further opportunity to get to the core of your problem.

PT: I don't try purposely, or I don't do it consciously.

TH: But let's focus on the issue of your not being specific, your being evasive. You leave every issue in the middle of nowhere and then I have to go back to the same question. And the most important question for both of us is, "Why are you evasive?" Because from what you have told me you have problems with men.

PT: Yeah.

TH: And you said you contradict yourself with your boyfriend and that he gets angry and has fits. And you have given me the picture that you are very disappointed in him.

PT: Yeah.

TH: Now my question is this: How about your relationship here with me? Obviously you have difficulties in life that are a source of agony for you. And now you have decided to do something about them. And I assume that you came here on your own volition, or didn't you?

PT: Yeah.

TH: Now if you continue to be evasive, as you know you do, then I will be useless to you and this session will be of no value to you. If we continue to skate around we cannot get to understand the problem; further, we will not be able to get to the core of your problem, something that we are here to understand. Do you see what I mean?

PT: Uh-huh. (*Silence*)

TH: You set up a goal for yourself . . . to come here, as you, yourself, put it, "to understand" yourself, to understand your problems with people. At the same time there is a paradox: Namely, by being evasive and vague you are in a sense defeating your goal. My question is, "Why do you do that?" Is this the way you are in every relationship? Is this your way with other people? (*Long pause*) What do you think? (*Long pause*) How do you feel right now?

PT: As though I have been scolded.

TH: In a way you didn't like what I said.

PT: That is how I feel.

TH: What do you feel inside?

PT: Kind of shaky.

TH: Do you feel irritated or angry?

PT: I did for a moment. But I listened to what you said, and you said it not as an accusation. Therefore, I didn't really have any right to feel angry.

TH: What do you think about what I said?

PT: Well, about setting a goal—and putting up a wall, or whatever, . . . well . . . that . . . uh . . . that has been for like . . . I have done it a lot. (*The patient is crying.*) This is a pattern of my life. I have done it in school because I have tried for an A, but I have always said to myself, "What the heck; I will probably never get an A, and don't be surprised if you don't—so don't get upset." So I don't know if I have ever really tried for an A. This self-defeating system is basically in every aspect of my life. I don't think I could really stand and really try for the highest. (*The patient continues to cry.*) (Davanloo 1980, pp. 106–109)

The next example shows Davanloo being supportive to the patient just after he has gotten her to admit that she was happy at the accidental death of her younger sister when the patient was 11.

TH: And that was the way to keep your secret. Let's look at your secret.

PT: That I might have been happy that she was dead.

TH: You say "might." Were you happy, or weren't you happy?

PT: Yes. (*The patient is crying and distraught.*)

TH: But of course this doesn't mean that you didn't also love her. And obviously you had some good things together. But what we have learned today is that your sister had certain advantages that you did not have. You were displaced from the front seat, you lost your pedestal, people preferred her for one reason or another, you had had all the attention for the first three years and lost all that, and then you had to get attention by being bad. So clearly you had a lot of feelings. (Davanloo 1980, p. 120)

In the final fragment from this patient, Davanloo links the patient's defenses against the therapist and her boyfriend to her defenses against her father (the T–C–P link). In response, the patient produces a confirmatory memory.

TH: But let's look at this nearly two-hour interview. Don't you think that you have been constantly putting up an iron wall around yourself and hiding behind it? And I have on many occasions had to dig and dig. I am sure that during this interview we have been able to break through some of these barriers, and we have touched on some very important issues; but it has at the same time been only with a great amount of digging. You are always hiding behind something. Is this passive way you take here with me, is this an expression of some hostility in relation to me?

PT: I know, I know, I know . . . okay. I can tell you. (*The patient is crying.*) I put up these defenses, like with my boyfriend. And I notice that I put up a barrier and don't let another person get to know me. I do it a lot. Perhaps you are right, that I resent opening up completely.

TH: Do you think that at one level it might have its roots in your relationship with your father, with whom you had a very close, intimate relationship? But then he changed completely.

PT: Uh-huh.

TH: At one time you left yourself open and were your father's "little Dutch girl," "little yellow bird." And suddenly he dropped you. Now you don't allow yourself to be open, and we have seen this all through the interview with me.

PT: All people.

TH: Of course. But I am specifically focusing on your relationship here with me and your need to put up an iron wall and not let yourself be open.

PT: Yeah.

TH: Do you think, then, there is a connection between this and your father?

PT: Yeah, I do.

TH: Huh?

PT: I do. I can tell you exactly when it happened, and what I said to myself. "I am never again going to get close to anybody." It was just after the automobile accident, and Becky was dead by then. My father and my sister used to stay at the hospital until late every night, and I was going to school. And I used to have to go to some friend's place after school. There were a few boys and girls, and I never felt comfortable there; and I worked. I used to do all the dishes and help do the cooking, do everything I could to earn my keep, or whatever it was there. And then I used to come home, and at first, for about two weeks after Becky died, I slept in the same bed with my father, where my mother used to sleep. And one night I was in bed, and my . . . this was actually on a Saturday, I think, I think it was . . . and Dad came upstairs and said, "Go to your own bed now." And I said, "Why?" He said, "Just go to your own bed." So I got up and left the room and went to my own bed, and I remember crying. And it was never the same after that. (Davanloo 1980, pp. 126–127)

THE MIDPHASE OF THE TREATMENT

During the midphase of the treatment there is less emphasis on the transference and more on the flow of material from the patient, which at this stage is quite rich. During the midphase of the treatment there is generally a good therapeutic alliance at work, and the patient is an active participant in the therapeutic process. The therapist, where possible, makes TCP interpretations. When there is resistance, relentless questioning is the most frequent technique used. Another prominently used technique is the frequent repetition of interpretations until the patient agrees. The therapist is alert lest the patient comply only for the sake of compliance, and if this occurs, it is, of course, interpreted. When transference resistances appear at this phase of the treatment, they are again clarified and interpreted. The full range of psychotherapeutic material available including memories, fantasies, slips, and dreams is used, although dreams and fantasies are generally not interpreted by using the patient's associations but rather by questioning the patient on particular aspects of the dream which he or she is asked to clarify. Davanloo is more aggressive in interpreting negative transference manifestations than he is in interpreting positive, particularly sexualized, transference manifestations, and when there is evidence of sexualized transference formation, he tends to be quite gentle with the patient, feeling that the patient would not respond well to harsh confrontations in this area.

The following example shows the richness of the material which often arises during the midphase of the treatment. The patient is a man in his early 30s.

PT: It seems our last meeting triggered a lot of memories.

TH: There was something about the last meeting that . . .

PT: Yeah. You remember I said I'd had a hard time remembering my youth unless we went backwards; but associations have taken place, and I've remembered certain things that I didn't remember last meeting. We talked about my father being away and coming home and being scared of him and all that. I seem to remember at some particular time feeling—I felt like I must have said to myself: "Thank God I don't have to be scared of him." I have that memory at some point when I was young—of feeling relieved that something had made me stop fearing my father.

TH: You said that last time you talked about the fear of your father, but what else did you talk about last time?

PT: About my mother, about wanting to see her body and her breasts and so forth.

TH: Your intense interest in the breasts and body of your mother?

PT: Yes.

TH: Now what happened when your father was away? He was away for twenty to thirty days at a time. What happened then to you, with all your interest in and fascination with the breasts of your mother and her body? Is there a relationship between that and your fear, since you had eyes, and you discussed also that when he was in bed with your mother, then the idea was that those breasts and that body were in the hands of your father?

PT: I don't remember feeling that. I remember—like I said, as we talk these things come back, such as the fact of the door being closed. In my mind all I see is a white door, and for that door to stick in my mind it must be what's on the other side of it that made me see the door; and on the other side of it was my mother, and I was not allowed to go in.

TH: What were your fantasies?

PT: I don't know what they were then. I really don't, because this was when I was five years old.

TH: But you had the memory about the breasts, didn't you?

PT: Yes, seeing her breasts feeding my sister.

TH: You also said that your interest was not in the feeding; that it was the breasts.

PT: Right.

TH: And you remember the white door?

PT: Yes.

TH: But you cannot remember anything in any fantasy about what was behind the door, yet also you remember your fear of your father. Do you see any connection between your fear of your father and your feelings about your mother? Was there a connection between the two? You were alone with your mother, and you were sneaking around to see her body when your father was not around. What sort of thoughts do you have about this?

PT: Yes, and that's the thing that triggered another memory about being very upset with my father. He came home from one of his trips and was to leave within a week or so, again to go away on business. Now, on this particular trip—I presume it was during the summer because he said he was going to take my brother away with him, and I remember very well trying to get in and say: "Can I go, too?" He promised he would take me, and I kept asking him because I guess I detected that his promise didn't seem to be very firm, and I kept asking him and he kept saying yes. So the morning of the departure, they didn't wake me up, but I was awake because I remember pulling the covers over my head and uttering obscenities, saying that it was a dirty trick and "How could you do this?" but I was talking to myself.

TH: But you were awake and you were pretending to be asleep?

PT: Yes, because I slept in a passageway where they had to pass back and forth as they were getting ready and eating breakfast. This is all going on very early in the morning, about 6:00 A.M., and he and my brother just went away and I was very upset. I remember that episode of pulling the covers over my head and swearing at my father, but I don't remember the week after when he was away. I don't remember that. That sticks in my mind.

TH: Are you saying that you really wanted to go with him?

PT: Yes.

TH: You say that you were awake and he had promised you, but you didn't announce that you were awake. You see, you were in bed and you pulled the sheet over your head so this brings the question really of whether you wanted to go away, or whether you were playing a trick with your father in your own mind, because if you wanted to go then you would get out of bed.

PT: I would think so now, but . . .

TH: So let's look at it. You said your father was playing a trick on you, but the question is really whether you were playing a game. Perhaps you wanted to go with your father, and perhaps also you were jealous of the close relationship between your father and your brother. At the same time, as we have seen, you wanted to be around the house with your mother; but finally the way you handled this conflict was to pull the blanket over your head and utter silent obscenities at your father.

PT: Could one come to this conclusion from one episode?

TH: Let us look at that episode, and then we will see. There you were, playing a game with your father in dealing with your dilemma. If you had really wanted to go, you would have gotten out of bed and said so.

PT: But I was scared of my father, too, at that time. If I had gotten out of bed, I don't know what he would have done.

TH: So we can look into that also. Let us go back to that because this is linked with other memories you have, namely, when your father was away, then you could be exclusively with your mother, and at the same time you have brought up fantasies of death wishes toward your father. Then there you were, wanting to be close to your father, and there are negative feelings you had toward your father, and you wanted to be around the house with your mother, her body, her breasts, and all of it. What thoughts do you have about this?

PT: Yes. Well, talking about the death wish is what made me think about that episode because that had been completely out of my mind for many years, although I can sort of recall having recalled it several times when I was younger. As the years went on I would say: "Gee, last year my father did that to me," or "Two years ago," you know, as I got older, but then there was a time when I didn't think of it any more. Another memory that came back when we were talking about breasts was a fantasy I used to have. I know I used to have it in that

same bed that I was in when my father went away without waking me. (*The patient is silent and appears very
uncomfortable.*) It's a weird fantasy. (Davanloo 1978, pp.
348–351)

This was followed by the patient remembering the details of a
fantasy that began when he was five or six in which he would
remove the breasts and genitals from a woman and place
them in a cement-mixer.

The treatment techniques for the more complicated and
sicker patients are the same as for the simpler cases, although
there will, of course, be much more resistance shown by the
more disturbed patients. In the obsessive and phobic patients
there is generally a large split between their affect and the
cognitive elements that relate to the affect. It is essential that
the patient experience his or her affect in a meaningful way
before further therapeutic work can be done, but with this
group of patients "bulldozer" techniques are often required.
By this, Davanloo means an even more persistent use of his
relentless confrontations of the patient's feelings, especially in
relation to the therapist.

THE END OF THE TREATMENT

By the fifth or sixth session one can begin to see evidence
of change in the patient, not only in the patient's relationship
to the therapist but also in the patient's functioning in his or
her everyday life. Improvement continues throughout the
course of the therapy, and when the symptoms which have
brought the patient into treatment have abated, the therapist
will ask if the patient has other issues he or she wishes to work
on for one or two sessions; if the patient has no other issues,
termination is initiated. By the end of treatment Davanloo
expects to see specific evidence of the "total resolution of the
central neurotic structure of the patient's problems manifested
by the total replacement of the maladaptive neurotic pattern
with an adaptive pattern associated with cognitive and emotional insight into the dynamic structure of his difficulties"
(Davanloo 1979, p. 21).

The following fragment illustrates how the therapist reviews the resolution of the chief complaints prior to termina-

tion. The patient came to treatment in a panic because marriage counseling was not resolving his separation from his wife. During the course of the treatment, the patient and his wife were reunited. He has just returned from a vacation with his wife.

PT: We went down to New Hampshire for two weeks. We very much enjoyed ourselves. We really had a good time. The weather was half and half, but we enjoyed ourselves very much. We got along very well together, and we had a pretty good time, you know, just being together, being close to each other—enjoying ourselves together.

TH: Then from what you tell me there are changes in your relationship with your wife?

PT: There was no flare-up; there was no problem of any . . . of even a minor nature.

TH: If you remember, when you first came here there was an obsession you had about your genitals. What about that?

PT: Oh. No. Oh, no. Our sex. When we were away on vacation we had very . . . oh . . . we had an intimate sexual relationship. The preoccupation with the size of my penis does not exist any more. I . . . uh . . . don't have a strong urge to . . . uh . . . be . . . you know . . . be screwing all the time. I feel more interested in other things now. There is no preoccupation.

TH: If you recall, when I first saw you you were disturbed about intruding thoughts related to homosexuality. Do you have such thoughts any more?

PT: No. I was very sensitive about it when we talked together. I guess perhaps I felt that it was a possibility, that there was something latent, you know, in my relationship with my father. It was a rather disturbing thought, but it is not there anymore.

TH: Now looking back, you have a mastery over many areas where you had difficulties. Is there any other area that you think we should continue to focus on?

PT: No. I was thinking tonight; and I came here with the intention of saying, you know, I feel that you can help other people in the same manner that you have helped me. I really have nothing but the greatest of, you know . . . affection and respect for your expertise. And I really want you to know that you have really helped me a lot. I feel I know myself; and what is to come for me I will deal with, and I can deal with on my own. Because anything that happens to me now . . . it happens to me, and I deal with it here. (*The patient is pointing to his head.*) I don't chase around and put myself in a bad position with other people and deal with it. I am straight-forward, and that is the way I want to be. And I really want to thank you for what we have accomplished. (Davanloo 1979, pp. 16–17)

When the core conflict is an oedipal one, the termination phase tends to be brief, usually occurring in one session. When the core conflict involves loss, or when there are multiple foci, the last two to six sessions are spent dealing with termination issues. As in other phases of the therapy, when termination is being considered, the therapist asks the patient to be specific. Davanloo has not run into the problem of regressive trans-ference formation with resulting difficulties in termination. He feels that this is due to his selection procedures as well as to the early and careful attention to transference formation, which when surfaced and clarified according to his technique serves to avoid the development of a regressive transference. No patient has unilaterally left treatment before its com-pletion.

When interviewed on follow-up examination, the patients remember therapy as gentle and helpful. They feel that they, the patients, did most of the work of the treatment. They often express feeling like a "free person" or a "new person."

PROBLEMS FOR THE THERAPIST

The practitioner of this treatment must have great sensi-tivity to what is going on with his or her patient. Particularly during the evaluation, before much historical information is available, care must be taken lest the confrontations lead to decompensation. As soon as the therapist is convinced that the patient cannot tolerate the confrontational technique, it must be discontinued and other modalities of treatment employed. Similarly, if during the ongoing course of the therapy there are signs of decompensation, the technique must be discontinued. Davanloo states that he has had no serious complications such as severe depression, suicide, or psychosis in any of his patients, but these dangers must be kept in mind, particularly by those less experienced or sensitive than Davanloo himself. Sensitivity is required not only to protect the patient, but it is also necessary in order to pick up the early and minimal manifestations of transference resistance on which this technique depends. If the therapist is unaware of these early resistances and waits until the phenomena are more blatant before intervening, the resistances will have become more firmly established and will not yield as easily to the therapist's intervention.

The therapist must also be comfortable with his or her own anger; otherwise, the technique may be used to express the therapist's own sadistic impulses, that is, to push the patient too hard, or, as is more likely, to allow the therapist, through a reaction–formation, to avoid the kind of confrontation that is necessary. In general, this technique requires a great deal of control on the part of the therapist. The therapist may often feel uncomfortable when affects similar to those being mobilized in the patient are stirred up within himself or herself. Any manifestation of these affects by the therapist such as responding with anger, coldness, seductiveness, or even playful good humor are contraindicated lest the therapist's response be too stimulating for the patient. Of all the techniques described in this book, Davanloo's requires the most consistent affective neutrality on the part of the therapist.

Doing this type of therapy requires time as well as emotional energy. Because of the speed with which phenomena occur during the course of the treatment, the only way the therapist can be in control is to be thoroughly prepared before each session. This means reviewing carefully the material of the previous session and hypothesizing about what is likely to occur in the session to come.

In addition to having a good knowledge of himself or herself and good control over his or her emotions, the therapist needs to be a good psychodynamic diagnostician. Much happens in a short period of time, and if the therapist is not skilled in reading the patient's productions and producing accurate interpretations, much valuable time can be lost. One of the techniques used is the repetition of interpretations, even if the patient disagrees with them; but if the interpretations are incorrect, they will obviously lead to difficulties.

TRAINING

Davanloo's is perhaps the most difficult of the brief psychotherapy techniques to learn. It requires the development of new techniques on the part of the therapist. The speed with which phenomena occur during this therapy is often confusing to the therapist. In addition, because the selection techniques are not as rigid as in some other brief therapy techniques, the therapist must constantly be on the alert for evidence that the patient is not tolerating the technique well.

Davanloo has a formal one-year training program for third- and fourth-year psychiatric residents and other experienced mental health professionals. The training consists of a didactic program including psychoanalytic therapy and technique. The main part of the program consists of groups of five students and an instructor viewing videotapes of actual treatments. All of the patients treated in the Montreal General Hospital with short-term dynamic psychotherapy have their complete treatment recorded on videotape, and these tapes are then used in the training program. Each student treats two or three patients by himself or herself. The supervision is intensive, the student receiving one hour of supervision for every hour of therapy for his or her first case, one hour for every two to three hours of the second case, and one hour for every five hours of therapy for his or her third case. The supervision is in the confronting style of the therapy, and the supervisor will challenge the student directly.

SUMMARY

Broad-focus short-term dynamic psychotherapy is a radical technique used to achieve extensive changes in a wide variety of patients, including some with long-standing obsessive and phobic disorders. Patients are selected if they meet criteria for motivation, intelligence, psychological mindedness, and ability to form object relationships. Most important is the patient's ability to respond to the trial therapy which is an integral part of the evaluation process. The trial therapy, and later the actual therapy itself, is characterized by the therapist's noting the earliest signs of resistance, particularly transference resistance, and confronting the patient with the resistance. As the patient is repeatedly and relentlessly confronted with the resistance, affect, usually anger, is mobilized. Further defenses to the affect are then produced by the patient which are then confronted by the therapist. After this process is repeated many times, new material is produced by the patient. The therapist links the material the patient produces in relation to the therapist with that produced in relation to significant people in the current life and significant people in the past (the T–C–P link).

Treatments last from 5 to 40 sessions depending on the complexity of the focus, the degree of psychopathology of the patient, the extent of the patient's resistance, and the experience of the therapist. Patients with multiple foci are treated. When the focus is an oedipal one, termination issues are not generally dealt with; for more complicated patients, the last sessions are used to deal with termination issues. No definite time limit is set. Treatment is ended when there is evidence of change in the patient's presenting symptoms, in his or her relationship to the therapist, and in relationships to others in his or her life outside the treatment.

Therapists practicing this technique need to be alert to what is going on with the patient at all times in order to be able to pick up the early evidence of resistance and in order to avoid confronting patients who are unsuitable for this technique. Therapists must also be comfortable with their own anger lest there be abuse or reaction–formation to the confronting technique employed. This is a relatively difficult technique to learn.

8

THE ECLECTIC SHORT-TERM PSYCHOTHERAPY OF WOLBERG

Wolberg has had 40 years of experience treating patients with brief techniques. As founder and director for many years of the Post-Graduate Center for Mental Health, a large mental health clinic and training facility in New York City, he has a wide experience with nearly all forms of treatment for a wide spectrum of patients, and he has brought this broad knowledge to his method of brief psychotherapy. Of all the techniques discussed in this book, Wolberg's is the least rigid and the most eclectic, utilizing nearly all the modalities of treatment available to the profession.

Wolberg organized a symposium on brief psychotherapy in New York in 1959. The papers presented at the symposium, including extensive discussions of technique by Alexander and Wolberg, were published in 1965. Wolberg (1980) recently published an expanded and updated version of his 1965 paper. While the other authors discussed in this book (with the exception of Alexander) have stressed specific selection criteria and then promulgated a fairly well defined set of techniques which are applicable to the selected population, Wolberg uses fairly broad selection criteria and then adjusts the technique to the individual patient as the treatment progresses and the characteristics of the patient become clearer to the therapist. Thus, there is not one short-term treatment technique of Wolberg, but there is rather a range of techniques and a strategy for employing them.

The goals that Wolberg strives for reflect the broad range of patients that he treats. He stresses that goals must be limited and realistic. He generally hopes to achieve symptom removal or amelioration; the return of the patient to his or her previous level of functioning; some intellectual insight into the patient's maladaptive patterns; and an ability by the patient to recognize his or her remaining maladaptive patterns and to develop some useful ways of dealing with these patterns in the future. In suitable patients reconstructive changes are possible, although he frequently stresses that one cannot hope to achieve the same results with brief therapy that one can in an ideal long-term therapy.

SELECTION OF PATIENTS

As part of the evaluation process patients are grouped into five classes. All patients are first given a trial of brief psychotherapy. For patients in Classes 1 to 3 this will be sufficient; patients in Classes 4 and 5 will require long-term treatment. Thus, a form of triage occurs as the therapist gathers information during the initial interviews. As more data become available, and as the therapist sees the patient's responses to his or her interventions, the diagnostic picture will become clearer, and the therapist will be able to formulate a definitive therapeutic plan.

Class 1.   This group includes those people who have had a generally good level of functioning until a recent decompensation occurred. The goal is to return the patient to the previous level of functioning; the techniques used are those of crisis intervention; and the length of therapy is from three to six sessions.

Class 2.   These are people who have disturbing symptoms or maladaptive patterns of behavior. The goal is symptom removal without insight (in contrast to Class 3 below). The techniques employed are "supportive–educational" and include such modalities as reeducation, suggestion, various behavioral techniques, and medication. The time frame for this treatment is 8 to 20 sessions. An example of a Class 2 patient is a person with an isolated phobia who is not psychologically minded or introspective.

Class 3. In this group are people who have symptoms and behavioral disturbances which can be connected to "deep-seated intrapsychic problems." In addition to the symptoms, these people will show signs of personality disturbances and inappropriate coping mechanisms. The goal is symptom removal and personality restructuring; the techniques used are psychoanalytically oriented psychotherapy with modifications as indicated; and the range of treatment is from 12 to 20 sessions.

Class 4. These people will be found to require further treatment during the course of the brief therapy. At what stage of the initial brief therapy this determination is made is quite variable. Sometimes the need for prolonged treatment can be established in one or two interviews; sometimes the factors that will call for long-term treatment do not become evident for some time. This group includes chronic psychotic patients who require ongoing contact and supervision; patients with a serious character disorder such as alcoholism who require long-term care and rehabilitative approaches; patients with uncontrollable acting out who need long-term controls; patients so "fixated" that they cannot function without someone on whom they can remain dependent; patients with chronic severe anxiety either because of a vulnerable ego or because of severe unchangeable reality circumstances; borderline patients; and patients with chronic intractable psychiatric symptoms that require continuous care, such as patients with severe obsessive–compulsive, paranoid, hypochondriacal, or depressive disorders.

Class 5. These are the people who want and can benefit from extensive "reconstructive personality changes," and who are realistically able to obtain long-term analytically oriented psychotherapy or psychoanalysis.

Because of the focus of this book, the remaining portions of this chapter will deal only with Class 3 patients.

THE INITIAL INTERVIEW

Wolberg emphasizes the importance of the initial interview. The initial interview will determine the fate of the therapeutic alliance and whether or not the patient returns for further therapy. From the beginning the therapist tries to convey to the patient a sense of optimism that the patient will be helped. The self-confidence and enthusiasm of the therapist is a powerful therapeutic tool and should not be hidden under the mantle of therapeutic neutrality. The therapist, by both attitude and responses, rapidly conveys to the patient a feeling of empathy, interest, and understanding. It is apparent that the therapist must be active from the very beginning. The therapist is also a good listener, and the patient is permitted to tell his or her story in his or her own way and is encouraged to express the accompanying affects. Wolberg believes that emotional catharsis is an important element in achieving therapeutic results.

The purpose of the initial interview is to engage the patient in therapy. It is not necessary to get a complete history during the first interview, since all patients are treated similarly at the beginning, but it is useful for the therapist to obtain enough information to make a tentative psychodynamic formulation. An attempt is made to relate the presenting problems with other symptoms in the past and with significant events in the patient's childhood. The patient is encouraged to make these connections on his or her own. This not only serves as a good measure of the patient's psychological mindedness and insight but also indicates to the patient early in the therapy that he or she will be expected to be an active participant in the treatment process. The psychodynamic formulation is generally presented to the patient in a fairly derivative form. Wolberg notes that too deep an interpretation in an unprepared patient can increase resistance and can lead to a discontinuation of the treatment. Unless the material presented by the patient clearly warrants it, and the patient shows a willingness and ability to deal with the material, deep interpretations should be avoided. Insofar as these patients have not been selected for their ability to deal with deep psychodynamic material, to err on the side of caution seems the prudent approach. As the therapy proceeds, and the therapist obtains evidence that the situation warrants it, the level can be deepened.

Resistances to the initial explorations are dealt with immediately, even if the therapist notes these at the beginning of the interview. Even transference resistances are dealt with at once. Thus the therapist is alert to any reaction the patient may show and can explore any difficulty he or she might sense. For example, if the patient is disappointed by the therapist's age or appearance, this should be discussed before other items are considered.

Once the therapist has a good understanding of what is troubling the patient, what the antecedents of the precipitating symptoms are, and what type of treatment is most likely to be effective, a verbal contract is made with the patient. In the contract the focus is agreed upon, and the patient is told that the treatment will be brief. If the therapist has a definite number of sessions in mind, this is told to the patient, and the termination date is noted. The patient is told that he or she will be expected to be active in the therapy and to work hard; at times the patient will be expected to do "homework" between the sessions. He or she will also be expected to work at putting into practice what has been learned. In this way the patient knows from the beginning that the treatment will not be merely an intellectual exercise.

Wolberg shows the patient Rorschach cards during the initial interview to help his diagnostic evaluation. Alternatively, Thematic Apperception Test (TAT) cards may be shown or the patient may be asked to draw a house, a tree, and a person. These simple projective tests are often helpful, but are certainly not essential in the routine evaluation.

The initial interview usually takes longer than 45 minutes and may be conducted over a period of several days. When indicated, family members or other important people in the patient's life may also be seen.

THE ONGOING THERAPY

As the therapy proceeds, the therapist looks for material that will help define the nuclear conflict and its derivatives in more precise terms. The most useful indicator of the patient's conflicts is his or her relationship with the therapist. The transference is carefully studied, but only interpreted when it becomes a resistance. It can also be used to show the patient how he or she reacts with significant people in his or her current and past life. The full range of psychotherapeutic modalities is used, including associations, fantasies, and dreams. However, in brief psychotherapy the therapist does not have the leisure to allow the material to unfold at its own pace and

so must control the flow of the patient's productions to maximize the benefit to the patient. Thus, only the parts of dreams
that fit in with what the therapist is working on are emphasized.
On the other hand, dreams can serve as a useful tool in helping
the therapist understand underlying dynamics and in evaluating the progress of the treatment. In a case reported in detail
(Wolberg 1977), the therapist was able to encourage the termination of the treatment after the patient reported a dream in
which she appeared with a full purse. In the same dream she
had a pleasurable sexual experience with a man. In a dream
from an earlier part of the treatment, she was alone and had
lost her empty purse. Associations to the earlier dream led to
an interpretation that she felt she had lost her femininity.

Generally it is most helpful to stay with the "here and
now." Dealing with the past without constantly relating it to
the current issues tends to promote regression and leads to
long-term therapy. It is usually enough to give the patient a
meaningful glimpse of his or her dynamics and to demonstrate
the patient's responsibility for the maintenance of his or her
distress. Confrontation is rarely indicated. In general, Wolberg
is supportive and tentative in his interpretations. He uses
humor as another technique to deflect the intensity of an
interpretation. While he works generally at a nonthreatening
level, he emphasizes that it is necessary to keep the tension
high throughout the treatment, and with some patients he
does achieve deep interpretations, including deep transference
interpretations, within the brief therapy time frame.

Whenever the opportunity arises, the therapist points out
that the main work of the treatment must be done by the
patient. It is the patient's responsibility to work out his or her
problems and apply his or her understanding to finding solu-
tions in the real world. The thrust of these interventions is to
keep the level of the tension in the treatment high while minimizing regression and dependence on the therapist.

Antianxiety medication can be used in conjunction with
the psychotherapy. Medication is indicated if the anxiety is so
great that it interferes with the patient's functioning. It is also
indicated when anxiety prevents the patient from trying out
new behavior, as for example before confronting a phobia.
For severe depression, antidepressant medication is used.

The hallmark of Wolberg's treatment is flexibility. Thus,
when a patient rejected a gentle attempt to work with the

homosexual content of a dream, the therapist switched approaches and encouraged the patient to seek a job. The suggestion to obtain a job was by no means capricious, but came from the therapist's understanding of the origins of the patient's low self-esteem and her previous history of having functioned well at work. Later in the therapy, the patient again brought in a dream and at that time she was able to utilize it. Wolberg is able to shift back and forth between analytic and supportive interventions in a rather special way, all the while keeping the transference under control (Wolberg 1977).

EDUCATION

While Wolberg eschews direct advice to the patient, he is very much the educator, teaching the patient first how to be a good patient and how to work in treatment, including explanations of mental functioning when indicated, and then teaching him or her how to conduct his or her life after the therapy has ended.

The patient is encouraged to practice self-observation both between sessions and after the therapy has concluded. In the beginning of treatment this consists of asking the patient to look at his or her current life situation and determine what he or she likes about it and what he or she would like to change. Similarly, the patient is asked to look at his or her patterns of behavior and determine which he or she would like to change and what new patterns he or she would like to acquire. As the treatment progresses, the patient is taught to look at the fluctuations of his or her symptoms and see if the fluctuations can be correlated with events in his or her current life. The patient is asked to monitor feelings of self-esteem and again try to note what causes fluctuations. He or she is asked to look at his or her relationships with other people on a daily basis. The patient is taught to observe his or her fantasies and dreams to see if anything can be learned from them, and is taught to look for resistances that arise when some of his or her new understandings are put into action. It is hoped that these patterns of self-observation will remain with the patient indefinitely. Continuing the self-observation, through means such as the relaxation tapes discussed below, not only serves as a useful tool for maintaining mental health but is also a way to continue the relationship with the therapist and thus make termination of treatment easier.

Wolberg teaches his patients what he calls a "more constructive life philosophy." He states that since all therapists implicitly convey their values to their patients, they might as well do so explicitly. His philosophy includes such items as learning to separate the past from the present, tolerating a "certain" amount of unpleasant affects, correcting remediable life situations and accepting the irremediable, using "willpower" to help control one's impulses, trying to control excessive superego demands, challenging diminished self-esteem, and deriving the utmost enjoyment from life. His advice seems to put the therapist in the role of the good parent helping the patient to mediate between the demands of the id, superego, and the external environment in a generally moderate way.

HYPNOSIS AND THE RELAXING TAPE

Wolberg uses hypnosis as an adjunct to brief psychotherapy, although he states it is not essential for the treatment and acknowledges that not every therapist will feel comfortable with it. Hypnotism, he says, is a catalyst for the therapy, helping to expedite it at various points. It is useful to increase the motivation of a patient; to provide symptom relief when the symptom is either incapacitating or so preoccupies the patient that he or she can do no work in therapy; to help start a relationship with the therapist when there is difficulty in this area; to help verbalization; to help explore a particular area where resistance is high; to help promote transference attitudes when they are blocked; to help recall traumatic memories; to deal with resistances to acting on insights; and to help with problems of termination.

The hypnotic process can also be useful as a means of eliciting transference reactions from, for example, the patient who is fearful of losing control or the patient who fears a sexual attack when being hypnotized. These reactions can then be used in the psychotherapy.

When properly used, hypnosis does not prolong therapy or lead to regression. Occasionally there is an intensification of the transference reaction. When this occurs, Wolberg stops the hypnotic part of the treatment and continues with the psychotherapy. Self-hypnosis can be taught to the patient for use after treatment ends.

Relaxing and ego-building tapes are cassettes made by the therapist which the patient uses twice daily. The tapes are made by the therapist in the presence of the patient, usually early in the course of the treatment. The content of the tapes consists of various relaxation and imagery exercises. The general aim of the tapes is to ameliorate symptoms, enhance self-confidence and self-understanding, and increase the patient's mastery over his or her environment. Wolberg states that the tapes reinforce the general message of the therapy, prove to the patient that something is being accomplished, intensify the relationship with the therapist, facilitate relaxation, improve the patient's self-image, and help with termination. Again, there is no evidence that the tapes increase dependency or regression. They do not interfere with the patient achieving a psychodynamic understanding of his or her problems.

THERAPY AFTER THE THERAPY IS OVER

More than any other writer in the field, Wolberg stresses the importance of the work that the patient does after the therapy has formally ended. He believes that most characterological changes that occur as a result of brief psychotherapy occur after the termination of the treatment. From the first contact with the patient he makes it clear that improvement is to be expected long after the therapy ends and that it is up to the patient to learn the techniques that will enable him or her to bring this about. As has been noted above, the patient is taught self-observation to enable him or her to be his or her own therapist, and is taught a new philosophy which can be applied to new situations as they are encountered. The patient is given the techniques of self-hypnosis and the relaxing tape to, in a sense, keep the therapist with him or her indefinitely.

Wolberg has no formal follow-up data, but he does mention informal follow-up visits of up to ten years which corroborate his belief that significant change occurs after the therapy had ended. Unfortunately, he supplies no information as to how his specific techniques contribute to these changes.

TERMINATION

Because of the factors noted in the previous section, termination is less absolute than in many other methods of brief psychotherapy. Of course, when the focus concerns separation, such issues are dealt with in the therapy. Sometimes it is useful to spread the last few sessions over several weeks to give the patient an opportunity to experience some of the separation feelings. Ideally, before the treatment is ended there should be a decrease in tension, a relief of symptoms, some insight, a proven willingness to try new patterns of adaptation, a greater capacity to handle frustration, a better mastery of the environment, a new outlook on life, and an increased ability at self-observation.

When the goals of the therapy have not been achieved in the allotted time and the patient does not clearly fit the criteria for long-term therapy, the patient is advised to see if his or her situation does not improve after termination. Contact with the patient is maintained on an infrequent basis, and, if necessary, another course of brief therapy may be attempted after several months if there continues to be no improvement. Even when goals have been achieved, Wolberg offers the patient the opportunity to return for a follow-up visit in the future if other difficulties arise. However, the patient is also warned that the vicissitudes of life are such that difficulties will surely be encountered in the future and that it is, therefore, important for the patient to continue practicing what has been learned in the treatment, even when feeling well, so that he or she will be better equipped to handle future problems on his or her own.

SUMMARY

Patients who, in the course of an extensive evaluation, are found to have symptoms or behavioral disturbances that can be connected to deep-seated intrapsychic problems are treated with analytically oriented psychotherapy for up to 20 sessions.

There is a wide variation of technique, which depends on the responsiveness and the needs of the patient, and ranges from a purely interpretive to a more supportive and educational one. Ancillary techniques including hypnosis, relaxation exercises, and drugs may be employed. All patients are encouraged to become more self-observant and to develop a good philosophy of life to take with them after the treatment has ended.

9

COMPARISON
OF THE VARIOUS
BRIEF THERAPIES

At the present time there are no studies comparing the particular brief therapy techniques discussed in this book with one another, nor are there any good studies comparing brief psychotherapy with long-term therapy. (Unfortunately, Strupp and Hadley's extensive controlled study of brief treatment [1979] did not employ any of the specific techniques described in this book; rather they relied on experienced long-term therapists to develop their own modifications of technique.) Thus, the selection of a particular form of brief therapy has to be made either on practical grounds, by what is available, or on the basis of a priori clinical reasoning and judgment.

Currently, there are few clinics or practitioners who are able to offer more than one form of brief therapy, so that, if brief therapy is indicated, the specific form of treatment that the patient will receive is often determined by who makes the referral or what services are provided by the clinic in the area. This is obviously unsatisfactory, and as more people are trained in the various techniques of brief therapy, it will become a practical as well as a theoretical problem to be able to determine which treatment is best for a particular patient. (It should be emphasized that in the following discussion of choice of therapy, it is assumed that the patient meets the selection criteria of the particular technique being considered.)

THE CHOICE OF BRIEF THERAPY

THE WORK OF BURKE, WHITE, AND HAVENS

The only attempt to compare the various brief therapies and provide a system for determining a treatment of choice that has so far appeared in the literature is the work of Burke, White, and Havens (1979). They provide a summary of the methods of Sifneos, Malan, Mann, and Alexander (and to a lesser extent that of Goldberg and Beck). They suggest that a rational choice of therapy can be made by understanding the developmental phase that is most prominent in the patient's conflict. Their thesis is that a different brief therapy is most apt for each developmental phase. Using the different stages of adult life proposed by Erikson, Levinson, and Vaillant, they indicate that a particular brief therapy is the treatment of choice, depending on the stage of development of the patient.

Burke, White, and Havens state that Mann's therapy is best suited for people struggling with the adolescent problem of identity versus role confusion, which is a recapitulation of the earlier separation–individuation phase of childhood. While Mann himself has stated that his treatment is particularly useful for people in late adolescence and early adulthood, he believes this is because that age group is struggling with problems of separation and that his method is particularly suited to deal with these issues. Burke, White, and Havens add to Mann's formulation the concept that Mann's approach is essentially an existential sharing of the patient's pain. Only by sharing the patient's feelings can the therapist reach patients at this particular stage of development. Passive–dependent patients especially will respond to the empathic therapist and recreate the "golden glow" of the first stage of Mann's treatment. Separation is then imposed from the outside by the therapist, just as weaning was imposed by the mother. The therapy is seen to work by providing a new and more positive introject, allowing for a more positive separation experience.

Certainly, there can be little argument that separation is a key problem for the above age group and that Mann's technique is designed to deal with problems of separation. However, when Burke, White, and Havens state that the existential approach is necessary for this group, that "to reach such a patient the therapist *must* [italics added] adopt an empathic approach," the argument is on less firm ground (p. 185). If there are data to support the conclusion, they are not cited by the authors.

Burke, White, and Havens generally group Sifneos and Malan together and suggest that their techniques are best suited to young adults struggling with the problems of "intimacy versus isolation," conflicts that usually express themselves in difficulty with heterosexual or peer relationships. These conflicts will often stir up unresolved oedipal conflicts, and these patients are often well suited to the interpretive styles of Sifneos and Malan. Burke, White, and Havens characterize Sifneos's and Malan's patients as hysterics who use repression as their main defense. The repression is undone through interpretations, the result of the therapist's "educational" efforts.

Burke, White, and Havens see Sifneos as the "unemotionally involved teacher," Malan as the "nondirective teacher," and state that the dramatic style of the hysterical patients responds well to the intellectual nonseductive style of the therapists. While certainly both Sifneos and Malan are nonseductive, it is difficult at times to see Sifneos as being unemotional. Of all the therapists discussed, he displays the widest range of affect in his work and, if anything, is more dramatic than most hysterics. Malan often does come across as the unemotional teacher, but Burke, White, and Havens's argument breaks down there because most of the patients described by Malan are not hysterics. All of the cases published by Sifneos are young adults, and many of them could be diagnosed as hysterics from the data presented, so that for Sifneos's patients, selected for their oedipal focus, there is a good fit with the developmental phases as presented by Burke, White, and Havens.

They find Alexander's techniques best suited for patients struggling with the midlife problems of "generativity versus stagnation." For this group they feel that the intellectual approach of Sifneos and Malan would only reinforce the patient's characteristic defenses and that the empathic approach of Mann would not find a sympathetic response. They state that the patient's primary conflicts at this stage of development center on problems of activity and that Alexander's active style of transference manipulation and his "managerial stance" foster the resolution of the patient's conflict in the direction of positive accomplishments.

Burke, White, and Havens's argument fits very well with the two cases in Alexander's book (A and B) that were treated by Alexander himself, but it ignores the wide range of patients of all ages and with various psychopathologies that are described in the rest of the book. They also minimize the extensive role of interpretation in the work of Alexander and his group, so that it may well be that Alexander's techniques are well suited to people with midlife crisis, but there are no data to indicate that they are not equally suited to others who meet Alexander's selection criteria. (Perhaps most of Alexander's patients were middle-aged because he was such a prominent clinician in his community that his practice attracted the most successful people.)

In addition to providing a rationale for choosing a brief therapy, Burke, White, and Havens also state that the concept of developmental phases might help explain the effectiveness of brief therapy. If the treatment is consonant with the developmental phase that is current in the patient's life, it might require only a small effort to enable the patient to complete his or her maturational tasks, freeing him or her to progress along the usual lines of development.

In summary, Burke, White, and Havens have provided a good beginning toward a system of classification of brief therapies. Like most such systems, their work suffers from the effects of oversimplification and the need to ignore important data in order to make the therapy fit into the classifications provided, but many of their ideas lay the groundwork for future studies, and some of their concepts are clinically useful at this time.

MATCHING THE STYLE OF THE PATIENT, THE THERAPIST, AND THE TECHNIQUE

A system of choosing the best brief therapy for a particular patient can be created using some of the elements proposed by Burke, White, and Havens but based on the match between the style of the patient, the therapist, and the technique rather than based on the developmental phase of the patient.

There is considerable literature suggesting that a good match between patient and therapist is an important determinant of outcome. It can be argued that the match between patient and therapist is more important in brief therapy than in long-term therapy. In long-term therapy, particularly when the therapist adopts a neutral stance, various aspects of the transference are projected onto the therapist during the course of the therapy. Provided the patient is able to tolerate the neutrality of the therapist at the beginning of treatment and stays with the treatment, the actual personality of the therapist becomes less important as the treatment progresses, since the patient will increasingly perceive the therapist according to his or her own needs at that particular time.

In brief therapy it is necessary for the therapist to be active from the beginning of the treatment. The activity of the therapist does not mean the abandonment of therapeutic neutrality, if by that is meant taking a neutral stance in regard to the patient's conflicts and real life decisions and revealing little about the therapist's personal life and values; however it is *not* possible to be an active and effective brief therapist and not reveal considerably more personality traits and characteristics than in a more classical analytically oriented long-term therapy. Therefore, the personality of the therapist will become evident to the patient from the beginning, particularly since in most of these techniques the initial interview is structured in such a way as to be a sample of the actual treatment situation. Thus, the personality of the therapist will become an important determinant of the formation of the therapeutic alliance and the course of the treatment.

In addition to matching the therapist with the patient, the therapist should be matched with the technique. One of the hallmarks of the brief therapist is his or her confidence in the technique. The therapist must be convinced, in order to project this conviction to the patient, that he or she will be able to help the patient accomplish the goals of the treatment in the allotted time. The confidence of the therapist will obviously be enhanced if he or she feels comfortable with the technique, and this will happen most easily if the technique is consonant with his or her own personality.

Of the techniques described in this book, perhaps the most difficult for therapists to learn is Alexander's manipulation of the transference. This aspect of Alexander's work has been least accepted, probably because it is so hard for most therapists to carry off convincingly. Because it has been rarely used, there is little information, other than Alexander's report, to indicate how important a part of the therapy the manipulation of the transference really is. In terms of the match of patient and therapist discussed above, the tailor-made therapist of Alexander is guaranteed to provide a perfect fit. If the therapist is both a skillful assessor of dynamics, so that an accurate picture of the ideal transference model can be quickly established, and a skillful actor, so that the transference model can be assumed and played with conviction, then Alexander's technique might be a suitable one for that therapist.

Sifneos's technique also requires skills which most therapists don't usually employ. The active, confronting, anxiety-provoking style of Sifneos is superficially very different from the supportive, helpful, and more passive role with which most therapists identify. Sifneos is actually more supportive than he seems at first glance, but the general tone of his therapy can be quite harsh at times. A therapist must be very comfortable with his or her own anger in order to be comfortable with this technique, so that he or she can use it freely in a therapeutic fashion, neither being overly aggressive, nor, via reaction–formation, being too passive. A flair for the dramatic also helps to speed along this treatment and helps to make it as affect-laden as it can be.

For Davanloo's technique, the therapist again needs to be comfortable with his or her anger. Davanloo's relentless pursuit of the patient's feelings and conflicts lends itself to the same type of distortions of aggression as do Sifneos's more openly aggressive maneuvers. However, for Davanloo's technique, drama is not only not required but is positively contraindicated. The therapist should be in absolute control of his or her own feelings, maintaining an affectual neutrality throughout, regardless of the material, lest the patient interpret the technique as either sadistic or seductive. In addition, practicing Davanloo's technique requires good clinical skills and intuition during the initial interview less inappropriate patients be selected.

Wolberg's technique requires a wide knowledge of ancillary approaches and a personality that is comfortable with a didactic, authoritative, and openly self-confident stance.

Malan and Mann's approaches are closest to the standard technique of the analytically oriented psychotherapist and require little modification. To practice Malan's technique, the therapist should be skilled in dynamic formulations and should feel comfortable making relatively deep interpretations. For Mann's technique, one needs to be, above all, comfortable with issues of separation as well as sufficiently empathic to determine the central issue during the evaluation period. Of all the techniques it requires the least confrontation.

It can be seen, then, that given a choice of techniques for a therapist and a technique most suitable for a particular patient, there should be a correlation between the style of the therapist, the style of his or her particular technique, and the personality of the patient. The exception to this would be if the therapist were skilled in Alexander's technique of manipulating the transference. Under these circumstances, as noted above, the therapist will create the match to suit any patient. With the other techniques, and with other aspects of Alexander's technique, certain of the patient's characteristics would lead to a particular choice of technique.

Thus, a passive, indecisive patient, whose chief problems center on a fear of lack of control of his or her impulses, might feel most comfortable with the paternalistic stance of Alexander or Wolberg, where the therapist is not afraid to take charge, give advice, and make decisions. This type of relationship would enable the patient to try new behaviors because he or she was "told to." The positive response the new behavior would receive, or more commonly, the lack of negative response the new behavior would engender, would then serve to reinforce the new patterns of behavior. A patient struggling with problems of adolescent rebellion would respond poorly to the same approach.

Passive–dependent patients will tend to do well with Mann's technique. As noted by Burke, White, and Havens, the dependency of the patient will allow the "golden glow" of Mann's first phase of therapy to develop to the fullest. This will set the stage for the subsequent disillusionment and prepare for a meaningful separation experience. In addition, the generally gentle technique will not stir up major resistances in the passive patient.

The "healthy" hysteric will do well with Sifneos's technique. The patient will respond to the dramatic confrontations of the therapist and will be spurred into a competition to outdo the therapist. If the therapy is properly structured, the only way the patient can beat the therapist is by coming up with bigger, better, more affect-laden, valid insights than the therapist can produce. But even this will not be sufficient, for the therapist will goad the patient to prove that he or she can employ the insights to change actual behavior. Thus, the only way the patient can win the oedipal fight with the therapist is to be "cured."

Davanloo's unique contribution lies in his ability to mobilize affect in patients who for many years have either repressed or isolated their feelings. Thus, his technique is particularly suitable for patients with obsessive and phobic symptoms, as well as those others who use isolation or intellectualization as their primary defense.

There is no one personality type that would do best with Malan's technique. Just as Malan's work, without much idiosyncrasy of technique, is in many ways in the middle ground of the techniques discussed in this book, so too most of his patients seem to have no one outstanding personality characteristic. His patients must have some ability to deal with intellectual insights and must be in touch with some of their important affects.

CHOOSING ON THE BASIS OF THE DEGREE OF HEALTH

It is possible to separate the techniques of brief therapy into the fixed and the variable techniques. Alexander and Wolberg have variable techniques in that they change their technique to suit the needs of a wide variety of patients. Sifneos, Mann, Malan, and Davanloo have a fixed technique; that is, they treat each patient in a similar manner and select those patients that they feel will be suitable for the technique. Among the fixed techniques it is possible to construct a hierarchy based on the health required of the patient before he or she can be selected for the technique.

The term "health," as used here, is determined after a composite evaluation of the patient's psychological functioning. Included in this evaluation are historical data on the patient's handling of age-appropriate tasks throughout development and the history of his or her relationships with people within and outside of his or her family. How the patient handled the various stresses to which he or she was exposed throughout his or her lifetime and any major episodes of decompensation are noted. The history of the patient's current symptomatology, and the history of symptoms which may have been prominent in the past but are no longer significant, are also recorded. The patient's current functioning is evaluated in such areas as work, the quality and stability of relationships with people, and the capacity to make use of leisure time in a pleasurable fashion. The range of the patient's affects and the quantity of affect available to him or her are measured. The flexibility and adaptiveness of the patient's character traits are evaluated. The patient's primary defenses are noted; their flexibility and the ratio of higher-level defenses such as altruism and suppression to lower-level defenses such as projection and denial are determined.

Alexander noted that the length of the therapy depends on the strength of the patient's ego. The stronger the patient's ego, the more the therapist can push the material while still achieving a therapeutic effect. If the therapist were to push material on a patient with a weaker ego, there would be "regressive evasion" which, of course, would not lead to therapeutic changes. (Assumed in this discussion is that the healthy patient is also psychologically minded and interested in understanding himself or herself. It is possible to postulate a relatively healthy individual who is so well defended that strong interventions by the therapist will lead neither to therapeutic change nor to regressive evasion. Such a patient would not be suitable for any of the insight-oriented techniques of brief therapy.) Sifneos's technique is based on these phenomena. He selects patients who are healthy and who, during the initial interview, respond to his particular technique in a positive manner. He then pressures them as much as possible and is thus able to achieve deep, long-lasting results in a very brief period of time, for example, 12 to 15 interviews. Malan's technique is less confronting, allows for the analysis of some defenses, and requires more time to achieve results which are similar to those of Sifneos. Malan's selection criteria, while still formidable, are less exclusive than those of Sifneos. With Malan, then, less health is required than with Sifneos. Mann's technique has the broadest selection criteria; that is, many more people will be suitable for Mann's technique than would be selected by Malan or Sifneos. In turn, Mann works at a more superficial level of insight, and his therapeutic claims are not as extensive as those of Sifneos and Malan.

There are advantages to using Sifneos's technique over that of Malan (e.g., the same results in half the time) and advantages to using Sifneos's and Malan's over Mann's, particularly if one believes in the therapeutic effectiveness of insight. Thus, if a patient is healthy enough to qualify, Sifneos's technique is the treatment of choice. If he or she does not qualify for Sifneos's method but does for Malan's, that becomes the treatment of choice, and if he or she qualifies for neither but does qualify for Mann's, then the patient will be treated with Mann's technique.

Davanloo does not fit into this neat classification scheme. He treats a group of healthy patients, similar to Sifneos's, with an oedipal focus in 5 to 10 sessions, or with a simple focus involving loss in 5 to 15 sessions, claiming results similar to those of Sifneos. But he also treats much sicker patients with a variety of psychopathology using the same technique, only the treatment will be longer, lasting up to 40 sessions, so that, according to Davanloo, his technique is applicable to all patients who are currently being treated by brief psychotherapy. The health of the patient and the complexity of the focus will determine the length of the therapy, not the choice of the therapy.

WHICH BRIEF THERAPY SHOULD A THERAPIST LEARN?

As was discussed, the most important element in choosing a technique is that the therapist be comfortable with it so that he or she can honestly convey the proper degree of confidence to the patient. But apart from considering which technique is most congenial to a therapist, there are practical considerations that might influence the therapist in choosing a technique to learn. Such considerations might include the availability of a particular technique of brief psychotherapy in the therapist's community or, even more importantly, the general applicability of a given technique. Davanloo has said that only 2 percent of patients seeking psychiatric help at the Montreal General Hospital, a large city general hospital, satisfy Sifneos's selection criteria. It is clear that Sifneos's technique has limited usefulness and that its usefulness will vary with the specific location of the therapist. Thus, if the primary responsibility of the therapist is to serve in a student mental health clinic in a large university, knowledge of Sifneos's technique will surely be clinically useful. If the therapist were serving in a rural Appalachian mental health center, it is likely that such a small percentage of his or her patients would qualify for Sifneos's technique that it would not prove to be an important addition to his or her armamentarium.

Davanloo claims that his technique has the widest applicability, that is, 35 percent of patients coming to Montreal General Hospital. (At the time of this writing he is experimenting with the use of his technique in the treatment of borderline patients.) Unfortunately, Davanloo has published the least data on his outcomes. Because his claims are the most radical and his work deviates in important respects from that of other workers in the field, it is difficult at this time to know how his technique will work in other hands. Malan, who certainly knows the field, is convinced that Davanloo's technique is valid and is the only brief therapy technique that needs to be learned. The techniques of Mann and Wolberg also have wide applicability, and Malan's technique, as usual, is somewhere in the middle. In any case, before a therapist expends the time and effort that are required to master any of these techniques, it is important that he or she consider what kind of practice he or she will have and whether the techniques make sense for that particular setting.

MIXING ELEMENTS OF THE
BRIEF THERAPY TECHNIQUES

Is it advantageous to take elements from one brief technique and use them as part of another technique? Is it advantageous to design one's own brief technique, assembling it from the elements presented by others? There are no good answers to these questions, as there are no data available. To some extent every therapist adapts a technique to suit himself or herself, but, as the techniques presented in this book have all been developed by individual therapists and tested using specific populations of patients, there certainly are some dangers in loosely mixing the elements of these techniques.

The most serious problem will occur if the correlation between depth of technique and selection criteria is disregarded. The depth and vigor with which interpretative psychotherapy can be pursued is very much a function of the health of the patient. If the patient is not able to tolerate the interpretations and is not so well defended as to be able to ignore them, then there will either be an increase in resistance, which rarely can be worked through during brief therapy, or there can be a major decompensation of the patient. (Malan [1976a] gives some clinical vignettes of serious complications occurring with improperly selected patients.) *It should be a firm rule that no element of a technique that was meant for a high-functioning patient be used with a lower-functioning patient.*

Similarly, the length of the therapy is a function of both the technique and the selection criteria for the patient. If an inappropriately short time period is set, the therapy will not be successful. Thus, if one is using Malan's technique and for external reasons sets a time limit of 15 sessions, rather than the usual 30, the results are likely to be poor, even though Sifneos can get good results in that time period. Mann's technique depends so much on the firm and irrevocable 12-session time limit that any change in that would invalidate his whole method.

There are other modifications for which the results are not so predictable. Can one use Davanloo's technique with a fixed time limit? Can one use Wolberg's technique of encouraging the patient to work on his or her problems after the termination with Malan's general technique? Can one use Alexander's manipulation of the transference with any of the other techniques? There are many combinations of this type where, on the one hand, there are no clear theoretical contraindications, and, on the other hand, there is no evidence that the modifications will not lead to a significant alteration of the basic technique. Table 1 represents an attempt to provide a rational basis for considering some aspects of mixing techniques. The following discussion expands on the data in the table.

Considering first the work of Alexander, it would seem that his method of changing the frequency of visits would be harmful in the other techniques, with the possible exception of Wolberg's, which may provide enough flexibility to encompass the change. In the other techniques, altering the frequency of the sessions could serve as a focus of resistance and, except as part of a termination procedure, is contraindicated. Alexander's manipulation of the transference, wherein the therapist assumes a role thought to be most beneficial for the patient, may not be compatible with the anxiety-provoking technique of Sifneos or the relentless pursuit of Davanloo. Mann's technique requires an empathic attitude which also does not lend itself to manipulation. Alexander's technique of encouraging the patient to experiment with new behavior in his or her real life outside of the therapy during the course of treatment can be applied with most of the other techniques. Depending on the particular transference that develops with Malan's technique, the somewhat authoritative stance that is necessary to make suggestions may interfere with the natural development of the transference. The other therapists assume a sufficiently authoritative or educational stance to permit suggestions to fit in more naturally.

While Sifneos limits his patients to those with an oedipal focus, any of the other techniques can be applied to a patient with an oedipal focus, though, if a choice of techniques is available, the question of which is the most powerful, that is, achieves the most long-lasting results in the shortest period of time, must be considered. Similarly, if a patient meets the rest of Sifneos's selection criteria, any of the other techniques are possible, though again, the most powerful available technique should be selected. Sifneos's anxiety-provoking techniques are obviously suited only to those patients who meet his stringent selection criteria.

Mann's technique is probably the least adaptable to others. The fixed 12-session time limit can be used only with his technique. The broad selection criteria allow patients to be treated with this method who would be excluded from the other techniques. Little is known of the effect of using Mann's central issue as a focus with the other techniques, but it would seem that it would lead to less introspection and less insight than a focus which is formulated in terms of intrapsychic conflict, so that the insight-oriented techniques of the other workers would probably be harmed by the use of the central issue as the focus.

Malan's selection criteria can be used with all techniques except for that of Sifneos, although Mann's technique would be the treatment of choice for a person meeting Malan's criteria only if separation is the main issue for the patient or if time allows for only 12 sessions. The question of fixed time limits is considered here. Though, again, there are little data on this question, it seems as though the matter of a fixed time limit

TABLE 1
MIXING ELEMENTS OF THE BRIEF THERAPY TECHNIQUES*

AUTHOR (NO. OF SESSIONS)	ALEXANDER	SIFNEOS	MANN	MALAN	DAVANLOO	WOLBERG
Alexander (2–65)	Flexible spacing of sessions	Encourage real-life changes	Encourage real-life changes	Manipulate transference	Encourage real-life changes	Manipulate transference / Encourage real-life changes
Sifneos (12–20)	Oedipal focus / Selection criteria	Anxiety-provoking attacks on defenses	Oedipal focus / Selection criteria	Oedipal focus / Selection criteria	Oedipal focus / Selection criteria	Oedipal focus / Selection criteria
Mann (12)			12-session time limit / Central issue / Broad selection criteria			

	Malan (20–30)	Davanloo (5–40)	Wolberg (12–20)
Malan (20–30)	*Fixed time limit*	Selection criteria	Selection criteria
Davanloo (5–40)		*Confronts anger and evasion / Treats severe psychopathology*	
Wolberg (12–20)	Self-therapy after termination	Self-therapy after termination	*Hypnosis / Relaxation tapes*

* Each author considered in this book is compared with the others. Where an important aspect of the technique of an author listed at the left can be applied to the technique of an author listed at the top, this is indicated in the section where the two authors' names meet. Those aspects of an author's technique which it is not possible to use with another technique are indicated in italics in those sections of the table where the author's name meets itself.

relates to the question of dealing with termination issues in the treatment. As has been most eloquently presented by Mann, setting a definite termination date brings up a great deal of material concerning separation in general. Sifneos, who limits his work to those with an oedipal focus and does little work with termination, uses a variable time limit. A fixed time limit would lead to separation issues and would necessarily prolong the treatment. Similarly, for Davanloo's healthier patients, where termination is not dealt with, a definite time limit would only prolong the therapy. A fixed time limit could be used with Davanloo's longer treatments where separation is often an issue. Alexander deals with separation issues by spacing the sessions, thus diluting the separation conflicts. This, of course, is the exact opposite of what occurs when a fixed time limit is used. Wolberg has used both fixed time limits and open-ended brief therapies, although he does not make his criteria for setting fixed time limits clear.

Davanloo, like Mann, uses elements which are quite different from the others and which make his technique difficult to use with the other techniques. Davanloo treats severe long-standing neurotic and characterological problems that would be excluded by the other workers. His confronting technique, both forcing the patient to avoid any vagueness and evasion and mobilizing and surfacing affect, particularly anger, seems to be such an integral part of his technique that it is difficult to isolate parts of it and apply them to the other methods. Of course, all therapists will ask the patient to be specific and all are interested in the patient's anger at one time or another, so that some of these elements will be found in any technique, but when they become the main focus of the therapy, then it is best to follow Davanloo's procedures in their entirety.

Wolberg's use of hypnosis and relaxation tapes has no place in the other therapies. However, his training of the patient to become his or her own therapist and so continue the therapy after the formal treatment has ended can be applied to other methods, except where issues of termination are central to the treatment. The continuation of the treatment by the patient tends to diminish the importance of the separation experience, and thus it would seem contraindicated when a fixed time limit is used and the separation issues are dealt with in the treatment.

In general, it would seem that at this time in the development of the brief therapies, unless there are clear indications for modifications, and the modifications can be tried on a large enough number of patients to make the results meaningful, it is best to adhere to one of the established techniques. While brief psychotherapy lends itself to research, it is certainly difficult for any individual practitioner to evaluate the complex variables involved. One of the drawbacks of doing brief therapy is that, in contrast to long-term therapy, there is rarely the time during the course of brief therapy to make up for the "mistakes" which variations in technique may have induced. If the therapist does not feel comfortable with any of the more rigid techniques described, the methods of Wolberg and Malan are flexible enough to provide a framework within which nearly everyone can work.

MIXING ELEMENTS OF BRIEF THERAPY WITH LONG-TERM PSYCHOTHERAPY

To discuss authoritatively the effect of bringing some of the elements of brief psychotherapy into a more traditional analytically oriented long-term psychotherapy requires a knowledge of the essential features of long-term therapy. This topic is obviously beyond the scope of this book and, unfortunately, at this writing is really beyond the scope of any book, insofar as the answers have eluded scholars and researchers who have struggled with this question for many years. It is of interest that Alexander was struggling with these very questions when he wrote his book on brief therapy, and his overambitious attempts to show what made any type of analytic therapy, including analysis, effective caused many of his valuable ideas to be rejected. Much of what Alexander described as techniques of brief psychotherapy became incorporated into the long-term psychotherapy that therapists practiced subsequently. Such modifications of analytic technique as working only with the latest relevant conflict, encouraging the patient to try his or her new knowledge in the real world, working through the conflict with other real people in the patient's life, rather than only in the transference, and varying the frequency of the sessions have become commonplace in long-term psychotherapy. These elements of brief therapy have enriched long-term therapy and made it more applicable to a wider group of patients, while at the same time shortening some of the treatments. Can some of the elements which the later workers in brief therapy introduced be similarly applied to the current practices of long-term therapy?

The answer to this question is, of course, not known. On theoretical grounds, it can be seen that the major problem of introducing brief therapy elements into long-term therapy is the change in the transference formation. One of the hallmarks of brief therapy is keeping the therapy at a level where regression is limited and the patient does not become dependent on the therapist and does not approach a true transference neurosis. In long-term therapy, the transference is allowed to develop more fully and on a more regressed level, and once this has occurred a shift to some of the elements of brief therapy can be expected to have untoward results. To use an extreme example, suppose that after two years of a traditional analytically oriented long-term therapy, the therapist shifted to Sifneos's technique of assaulting the patient's defenses rather than continuing to analyze them as the therapist had been doing. The patient would undoubtedly experience this as a severe and surprising attack, and it would be unlikely to be therapeutic.

There are, however, elements of each brief therapy technique which might be used in long-term therapy with a greater likelihood of success. Alexander's contributions have already been noted. While Sifneos's general technique is probably not applicable to long-term therapy, his therapeutic stance, that is, applying as much pressure to the patient as is safe, is a good principle for long-term therapists that is often overlooked. Alexander made a similar point earlier, but Sifneos has really shown that many patients can tolerate a great deal more stress in the treatment than was heretofore thought optimal. The general tendency of long-term therapists to let the material flow as it may has needlessly prolonged many a therapy. Even when long-term therapy is clearly indicated, keeping the level of tension high is often productive in properly selected patients.

Mann has made the point that many long-term therapies end without adequate preparation for separation, and his emphasis on this aspect of treatment should be incorporated into every long-term treatment. Except for the sudden refusal of a patient to continue the treatment and his or her refusal to discuss it, or the sudden incapacity of the therapist, there are no reasons why termination issues cannot be dealt with in every long-term treatment. Mann's formulation of the "central issue," that is, the empathic response to the "chronic pain" that the patient experiences, is also something that any therapist can incorporate into his or her technique, regardless of the length of the treatment.

Malan, like Sifneos, has shown that patients can often absorb much more than therapists had assumed, and his ability to make deep interpretations early can also be used in longer treatments. The key to the successful use of rapid interpretation in long-term psychotherapy is recognizing when the patient is really ready to deal with the material rather than using the interpretations as a means to intellectualizations or as a defense against dealing with other, more important material.

Davanloo's pursuit of the patient's feelings, particularly his or her anger, probably has wide application in long-term treatments. The emphasis on feelings to the exclusion of content has characterized some fringe therapies that have appeared in recent years, but Davanloo is able to combine the expression of feelings with the appropriate content to create a meaningful therapeutic experience. How relentless a therapist can be in a long-term treatment situation without stirring up counterproductive masochistic and other fantasies in the patient remains to be discovered.

Much of Wolberg's technique of brief therapy came out of his own long-term work; so his brief and long-term techniques are quite similar. A generally applicable technique involves teaching the patient to be responsible for his or her own behavior and role in the therapy. If used injudiciously in a long-term treatment, this attitude can stultify the development of the transference and lead to power struggles between patient and therapist, but too often in long-term therapy the therapist allows the patient to develop the idea that the only responsibilities that the patient has are to come, pay the bill, and speak his or her thoughts. When this attitude exists, treatment tends to be endless and real change rarely occurs.

In general, if there is a strong therapeutic alliance, and the therapist has a good understanding of the patient and of the status of the transference, the type of modification of long-term therapy technique that has been discussed above can be attempted with little danger. If the attempts at modification of technique are unsuccessful there will generally be an opportunity to make the appropriate corrections.

10

THE RELATIONSHIP BETWEEN BRIEF PSYCHOTHERAPY AND CRISIS INTERVENTION

In an old story about an ocean voyage to the Far East the only nonwhites among the first-class passengers were two Chinese men who were always seen walking on the deck together. When one night one of the Chinese men became severely ill, some of the other passengers solicitously broke the news of the illness to the other Chinese man. The passengers were stunned by the second man's indifference. It turned out the two men were not friends, but that they only walked together because no one else would talk to them. So it is with brief psychotherapy and crisis intervention. They are frequently seen together in the literature, and clinicians who know little about these modalities think they are quite similar, while in reality they have little in common except for the superficial attribute of brevity. This chapter will delineate the differences and similarities between brief psychotherapy and crisis intervention to provide a clearer picture of their distinct aspects and the usefulness and limitations of each modality of treatment.

HISTORICAL ASPECTS

In this section, the history of the relationship between psychoanalytically oriented individual brief psychotherapy and crisis intervention will be discussed. There will be no attempt either to review the history of crisis intervention in general or to consider the nonanalytically oriented brief psychotherapies that grew out of the concepts of crisis intervention.

Present-day crisis intervention dates from the studies by Erich Lindemann (1944) of survivors of the devastating Coconut Grove nightclub fire in Boston. Writers on brief psychotherapy before that time, including Alexander, who did most of his work on brief psychotherapy before 1944, did not consider the question of crisis intervention in relation to their own work. However, later writers on brief psychotherapy were strongly influenced by the impact of crisis intervention on the mental health movement. Thus, Malan's review (1963) of brief psychotherapy before 1960 did not mention crisis intervention, while his review (1976) of brief psychotherapy after 1960 contains an extensive discussion of the relationship of these treatment modalities. By the 1960s crisis intervention was established as a useful modality of treatment. Federally funded mental health centers were required to have facilities for emergency treatment and crisis intervention, so that at a time when brief psychotherapy had little legitimacy and support, crisis intervention was a recognized way of helping people. Malan points out that, as a result of the success of crisis intervention in producing permanent changes in people with acute problems, the climate became more favorable for the acceptance of the idea that people with long-standing problems could also be helped by brief interventions.

Of the writers considered in this book, Sifneos is the only one who had wide personal experience with crisis intervention before he developed his technique of brief psychotherapy. (One of Sifneos's early criteria of selection for brief psychotherapy was that the patient be in an "emotional crisis," although he later abandoned this criterion because too few patients were available to fulfill it. It was only after he abandoned this requirement that he realized it was not necessary.) His early published work on brief psychotherapy (Sifneos 1967, 1972) included considerable material on crisis intervention. Indeed, in these publications he presented a system of classification of brief therapies that included both brief psychotherapy and crisis intervention. He divided brief therapies into anxiety-provoking psychotherapy and anxiety-suppressive psychotherapy. Anxiety-provoking psychotherapy consisted of the short-term anxiety-provoking psychotherapy as described in Chapter 4 and crisis intervention. Anxiety-suppressive psychotherapy consisted of brief anxiety-suppressive psychotherapy and crisis support. Anxiety-provoking therapies were for generally healthy patients, while the anxiety-suppressive techniques were for those patients who did not meet the criteria for anxiety-provoking therapies. For Sifneos, crisis intervention was a technique for people who, in general, met the selection criteria for short-term anxiety-provoking psychotherapy and who were in an "emotional crisis," which he defined as an "intensification of a painful state which has the potential of becoming a turning point for better or worse" (Sifneos 1967, p. 1071). The details of Sifneos's technique of crisis intervention are not discussed here, but it is important to note that his classification of brief therapies, in particular his definitions of crisis and crisis intervention, have not been generally accepted by workers in the field of crisis intervention.

Caplan is the generally accepted theoretician of crisis intervention. He defines a crisis as the result of a situation where "the individual is faced by stimuli which signal danger to a fundamental need satisfaction or evoke major need appetite, and the circumstances are such that habitual problem-solving methods are unsuccessful" (Caplan 1964, p. 39). Once the individual finds himself or herself in this situation there will be a rise in tension which calls forth new problem-solving techniques. If these new techniques are successful, the problem is solved, but if they are not successful, tension continues to rise, producing a characteristic state in the patient consisting of feelings of anxiety, fear, guilt, shame, ineffectuality, and helplessness. If no solution is provided, the tension may increase until there is disorganization of the personality. It is the subjective feeling by the individual that he or she is faced with a serious problem with which he or she cannot cope, *regardless* of what he or she tries to do, that constitutes the crisis.

While Caplan's definition may be somewhat rigid and restrictive, it has the advantage of being specific enough so that most observers can agree as to when a patient meets the criteria. In addition, as will be seen later in this chapter, Caplan's definition generates certain theoretical concepts and treatment strategies, leading to a unified theoretical and clinical picture of crisis intervention. In contrast, Sifneos's definition of an emotional crisis as an "intensification of a painful state which has the potential of becoming a turning-point for better or worse" is much broader. While he recognizes that unsuccessful attempts to master the situation are part of the crisis picture, he does not make it an essential part of the definition; so many situations would be considered a crisis by Sifneos that would not meet Caplan's criteria.

Sifneos's definition of crisis continues to exert some influence on writers on brief psychotherapy. The result of using Sifneos's definition, rather than Caplan's, is that the distinction between crisis intervention and brief psychotherapy becomes much less clear (Marmor 1979). Rather than describing two discrete modalities of treatment, the use of Sifneos's definition promotes the idea of a therapeutic continuum along which one may find both crisis intervention and brief psychotherapy. (In this vein, for example, Malan suggests that in many situations the word "crisis" can be replaced by "current conflict"; by changing the name of the presenting situation, crisis intervention is changed into brief psychotherapy.)

The Third International Symposium on Short-Term Dynamic Psychotherapy held in 1977 included a section devoted to crisis intervention (Davanloo 1980). The contributors to this volume show the confusion that was prevalent in the field by that time. Straker seems to find little difference in selection and technique between brief psychotherapy and crisis intervention, Davanloo and Sifneos demonstrate minor modifications of their brief psychotherapy techniques and call them crisis intervention, while Marmor presents an extensive and lucid differentiation of the two modalities.

As will be demonstrated, there are both theoretical and practical advantages to separating crisis intervention from brief psychotherapy. In order to make this distinction clear, Caplan's definition of what constitutes a crisis will be used in the following discussion.

PRINCIPLES OF CRISIS INTERVENTION

In order to compare brief psychotherapy and crisis intervention, it is helpful to review the basic elements of these techniques. Brief psychotherapy was discussed in Chapter 1. For those unfamiliar with the techniques of crisis intervention, crisis intervention will be briefly reviewed here.

As was noted above, the techniques of crisis intervention follow from the definition of what constitutes a crisis. Since the chief subjective affect of being in crisis is a profound sense of helplessness, the chief aim of crisis intervention is to eliminate the feeling of helplessness and enable the patient to experience a feeling of mastery over the situation that had previously defeated him or her. As Caplan has emphasized, the opportunity to achieve mastery can have far-reaching consequences for the patient, for not only can the patient be returned to his or her previous level of functioning, but, because mastery of a difficult situation often leads to the incorporation of newly acquired coping mechanisms, increased self-esteem, and less fear of future traumata, the patient can emerge from a successfully handled crisis with improvements that will, in turn, favorably affect other areas of his or her life. (The Outward Bound program, where individuals learn to cope with hazardous natural environments as a way of promoting personal growth and building inner strength, is an institutionalized attempt to achieve feelings of mastery by creating a manageable crisis for the participant.)

There are no criteria for selecting a patient for crisis intervention other than that the patient be in crisis. According to the view presented here, diagnosis, previous level of functioning, or measurements of ego-strength are not relevant as selection factors. (If the definition of crisis as awareness of lack of coping mechanisms is remembered, it will be seen that most psychoses do not fit the definition. The psychotic symptoms themselves generally help to defend the patient against feelings of helplessness.) There are many factors which determine whether a given individual will experience a crisis. There are external factors such as a major disaster or prolonged combat which elicit feelings of being in crisis in a majority of participants. There are other events, such as the death of a loved one or transition states such as retirement, that will be stressful for most people but will elicit crisis states in relatively few. Cultural factors also determine what will be stressful for a given individual, but the most significant determinant of a crisis is the past history of the individual. Most crises are a combination of an external stress interacting with a particular vulnerability based on the past experiences of the individual.

The techniques of crisis intervention are designed to enable the patient to gain control over the crisis situation. While the various factors will be discussed separately, it is apparent that there is no fixed order of intervention, and several types of interventions may be used simultaneously. Probably the single most important therapeutic factor in crisis intervention is the patient's relationship with the therapist. Because the patient feels helpless as a result of the crisis, he or she will be more ready than usual to accept help from another. Also, because the patient feels helpless and defenseless, he or she will tend to be regressed, so that a rapid, and often a deeply dependent, therapeutic relationship can be formed with a patient in crisis. The rapid establishment of this relationship often leads to the quick amelioration of symptoms, as the patient now no longer feels helpless, but rather experiences the therapist as a strong and powerful helper who will resolve the crisis for the patient. The crisis therapist must be careful to use the therapeutic relationship as a means of helping the patient achieve a sense of mastery rather than as a means of promoting the patient's dependence. Toward this end, the therapist should present himself or herself as confident and in control, while being careful not to be controlling and authoritarian. While the therapist must, of course, be active, the *least* amount of activity that is necessary to enable the patient to regain control should be used (Flegenheimer 1978).

Once contact has been made, it is important to identify and clarify the elements of the crisis situation. Often the patient feels so overwhelmed that he or she can no longer distinguish the various factors impinging on him or her. Being able to see the crisis clearly is a step toward achieving an intellectual grasp of the situation, which in turn helps the patient to achieve a sense of control over the problem. It is apparent that the more that is known about the patient, the easier it will be to make a meaningful intellectual formulation of the crisis. Thus, if it can be established that a man is in crisis because of a threat of the loss of his job, this will be helpful to him, but it will be much more helpful if it is known and can be presented to the patient that his current reaction is related to his childhood and adolescent struggle with an overbearing father who predicted that he would never be a success. This brings up one of the chief technical problems in doing crisis intervention. On the one hand, in order to establish a meaningful relationship with the patient, the therapist must be empathic to the patient's immediate needs, which are nearly always focused on the present crisis. On the other hand, in order to be of most help, the therapist must have a good understanding of the important elements which led to this particular crisis, and this requires knowing something of the patient's past. It is the skill of the therapist which enables him or her to know when it is possible to shift from the present to the past and gather the necessary information while still conveying an understanding of the patient's current suffering. It is easier to accomplish this when large blocks of time are available, particularly for the initial meetings, so that both the past and present can be attended to in the same session. When this is not possible, frequent visits, especially at the beginning of the crisis treatment, are helpful.

Permitting and encouraging the patient's ventilation of affect is another feature of crisis intervention. Here the accepting and nonjudgmental stance of the therapist is crucial, as is the ability of the therapist to control the flow of the affect lest the patient become frightened of losing control when his or her feelings become very intense. It is often helpful to let the patient know that intense affect is not necessarily a sign of insanity. It is rarely necessary or even advisable in crisis intervention to uncover repressed affects. Generally the patient has too much affect to deal with; so bringing forth additional feelings, for example, the unconscious anger behind the feelings of loss, is rarely indicated during the acute phase of the treatment. The one exception is when there is an obvious, massive denial of feelings, such as when there is a denial of a real loss; then it is necessary to help the patient break through the denial and become aware of the appropriate feelings.

Similarly, interpretation or analysis of the patient's defenses is rarely indicated during the acute phase of crisis intervention. The crisis is the result of the patient's having too few defenses, and what few he or she has left are probably needed. Rather, the task of the therapist is to enable the patient to develop new defenses and coping mechanisms which will help him or her through the crisis. Interpretations which tend to increase the level of anxiety and, therefore, the stress on the patient are usually not given, except when they are used to relate historical material to the present crisis in order to help the patient understand the intensity of his or her current reactions. Sometimes the therapist will suggest coping mechanisms that the patient has not thought of, but this is usually not necessary since providing the proper therapeutic milieu often removes sufficient pressure from the patient so that the patient himself or herself can devise a solution that has heretofore been overlooked to the particular problem. Ancillary sources of help such as family, friends, and community resources are employed as indicated. Often the task of the therapist is to smooth the way between the patient and others so that the patient's natural support network can be reestablished. When other resources are unavailable, the therapist may have to help in providing concrete services to the patient. Medication and partial or temporary hospitalization may also be used to reduce the pressures on the patient and permit the development of new coping mechanisms.

While some workers use a fixed number of sessions, for example, six, others do not, and a fixed number of sessions or a fixed time limit is not an essential feature of crisis intervention. It is important, however, that the patient be told early in the treatment that the therapy will be a brief one so that the patient, as well as the therapist, can be on guard against excessive feelings of dependency. The crisis treatment is ended when the crisis is over and the patient has reestablished equilibrium. Most crisis therapy consists of six to ten sessions over a four-to-six-week period. At times, as a result of what has been learned during the crisis treatment, the patient will want to proceed with other forms of psychotherapy. More often, however, no further treatment will be wanted or indicated. If there is to be no further therapy, it is important that the patient knows that the door is open, that is, that the patient knows that there has been no definitive solution of all his or her conflicts and that, if further help is required in the future, he or she will be welcome to return. The patient should leave treatment with positive feelings for the therapist and the institution intact in order to make it easier for him or her to return. Hence, it is inadvisable to pressure the patient into further treatment at the end of the crisis if the patient is genuinely not interested. When the patient feels that the therapist wants him or her to stay for further treatment, the patient will usually leave therapy with the feeling that he or she disappointed the therapist; much of the increase in self-esteem which the patient may have achieved as a result of the crisis intervention can be lost in this way.

THE COMPARISON OF CRISIS INTERVENTION AND BRIEF PSYCHOTHERAPY

Marmor (1980) has compared brief psychotherapy with crisis intervention, and his work was used as the basis of Table 2. The following discussion expands on the data in the table.

The selection criteria and the selection process are radically different in the two modalities of treatment. Careful selection is an absolute requirement for any brief psychotherapy. The initial interviews are used to acquire sufficient information for a careful diagnostic and psychodynamic assessment of the patient. Perhaps even more important, the initial interviews are used as a trial therapy, so that at the end of the evaluation period the therapist is in a position to make a good prediction as to whether or not the particular patient will do well with the particular method of brief psychotherapy being considered. In order for the patient to meet the requirements of the evaluation process, he or she must be able to give a coherent picture of present and past difficulties, must demonstrate an ability to relate to the therapist in a meaningful fashion, and must agree to a treatment contract. In most settings there is a wait until the first evaluation interview can be arranged, and, because the evaluation process frequently requires more than one interview, there will often be an additional delay before the therapy actually commences. The patient must be able to tolerate these delays without serious ill-effects. While the brief psychotherapies do not have selection criteria based on diagnosis, the selection criteria are such that patients chosen will generally have either a mild or moderate neurotic disorder or a mild personality disorder. Patients who meet the diagnostic criteria for more serious disorders are rarely accepted for brief psychotherapy.

On the other hand, the only requirement of a patient for crisis intervention is that he or she be in crisis. This can usually be determined rapidly by the therapist, and a full history and a full assessment of the strengths and weaknesses of the patient, while of course helpful, are not necessary before the crisis intervention commences. Crisis intervention can be utilized with patients with *any* diagnosis ranging from acute situational reaction to chronic schizophrenia, as long as the

TABLE 2
COMPARISON OF CRISIS INTERVENTION WITH BRIEF PSYCHOTHERAPY

	CRISIS INTERVENTION	BRIEF PSYCHOTHERAPY
Selection	Any diagnosis; must be in crisis—no other selection criteria	Mild to moderate neurosis; mild personality disorder; specific selection criteria
Onset	Recent	Can be long-standing
Focus	Immediate stress	Core conflict
Goal	Restore homeostasis; promote mastery	Symptom amelioration; promote more adaptive coping mechanisms
Technique	Supportive: promotes defenses; may be directive; rarely interpretive	Confronting: removes defenses; nondirective; interpretive
Structure of Therapy	Flexible: rapid onset of treatment; one-to-one plus others; sessions of variable length and frequency	Structured: extensive evaluation period; one-to-one; sessions of standard length; one session per week
Transference	Initially regressed; transference interpretations rarely used	Level of regression controlled; transference interpretations common
Termination	When crisis resolved, usually 6–10 sessions; may have time limit; termination issues often not discussed	At end of time limit or when conflict resolved, usually 12–30 sessions; termination issues often discussed

Adapted from Marmor (1980).

186

defenses of the patient at the time of presentation are fairly
fluid and the patient experiences the subjective feelings of the
crisis situation. Crisis intervention may be suitable for a patient
regardless of socioeconomic status, level of education, level of
previous functioning, psychological mindedness, or intelligence. The assets that the patient brings to the treatment will
help determine the level at which the therapy will proceed,
but the absence of these assets does not preclude a successful
resolution of the crisis.

While crisis intervention is suitable for a broad range of
patients, it is usually necessary for the patient to come to the
therapist fairly soon after the onset of the crisis. Because of the
intensity of the feelings experienced during the crisis, the patient is unable to maintain himself or herself in that condition for any length of time, and so some sort of resolution of
the crisis usually occurs with or without treatment. Without
the proper help, however, the resolution is often a maladaptive
one for the individual or for those around him or her. (Occasionally one may see a patient who has not come for help and
who is able to maintain himself or herself in a state of crisis for
some months, but this is unusual.) With brief psychotherapy,
of course, there is no such requirement for rapid intervention,
and people with long-standing symptomatology can be treated.
The focus of crisis therapy, once the treatment has begun,
remains on the current acute stress, with past material being
brought in only to help clarify and explain the current crisis.
With brief psychotherapy the focus is on a long-standing con-
flictual situation, related as closely as possible to the patient's
core conflicts.

The goal of crisis intervention is to restore the patient to
his or her previous level of functioning. It is hoped that the
patient will learn new coping mechanisms and will come
away from the treatment with an increased sense of self-
esteem based on successful mastery of the crisis. While a
successful crisis experience may have a long-range, beneficial
effect on the patient's life, no attempt is made during the crisis
therapy to have the patient understand any of the core conflicts. In brief psychotherapy the aim is to have the patient
gain an intellectual and affective appreciation of his or her
conflicts in order to help bring about changes in the patient's
life. Looked-for changes include symptom amelioration, some
characterological changes, and shifts in the patient's coping

mechanisms, including shifts in defense mechanisms, to a higher level of adaptation.

The technique of crisis intervention is essentially a supportive one. The therapist presents himself or herself to the patient as a concerned helper, and, while the therapist tries to shift as much of the burden as possible onto the patient, the crisis situation is such that the therapist often has to do much of the work of the treatment. While affect is accepted, there is little attempt to uncover repressed affects. Defenses are shored up, and help is given the patient in finding new defenses. Interpretations are rarely given and are indicated only to help elucidate the antecedents of the crisis. At times the therapist may be frankly directive and may even engage in such activities as accompanying the patient in some essential task, for example, applying for emergency welfare benefits, if it is felt that the patient cannot accomplish the objective on his or her own and there is no one more suitable available.

In crisis therapy the crisis situation itself produces an excessively high level of tension in the patient, and the task of the therapist is to reduce this tension so that the patient can regain control; in brief psychotherapy one of the chief tasks of the therapist is to engender and maintain a sufficiently high level of tension in the patient so that the therapy can proceed at an optimum level. The brief therapist uses a variety of techniques including interpretation, confrontation, interpreting or attacking defenses, and persistently attempting to mobilize the patient's affects to keep the tension high. Interpretations are also used to help elucidate the focus and to bring repressed affects and memories into the treatment. While the therapist may at times be supportive, the support is used to regulate the level of the tension and is never the primary modality of treatment. The brief therapist rarely needs to be directive.

Brief psychotherapy is a fairly rigidly structured treatment. The therapy is conducted on a one-to-one basis, the sessions are regularly spaced, usually on a weekly basis, and each session generally lasts the same 45 or 50 minutes each week. In contrast, one of the hallmarks of crisis intervention is its flexibility. The therapist is not restricted to seeing only the patient. Indeed, it is usually helpful, particularly in the beginning of the crisis treatment, to see as many people accompanying the patient as possible. Subsequent interventions with family members, friends, or others in the patient's life are often helpful. Crisis sessions need not be scheduled on a regular basis. Initially, daily visits may be necessary, but the frequency can often be rapidly decreased, with extra sessions added as indicated. Telephone contacts between sessions are often used. The sessions may be of variable length. The first visit may last two to three hours, other sessions may last 45 minutes, and at times brief sessions lasting 5 to 10 minutes may be helpful to monitor the progress of the patient.

The vicissitudes of the transference formation are quite different in the two modalities of treatment (Flegenheimer 1979). The initial reaction of the patient in crisis to the therapist is determined by the feelings which the patient brings to the situation. As a result of feeling helpless and unable to cope, he or she is both ready for help and regressed to such a level that a rapid, intense, regressively tinged transference is formed at the beginning of the crisis treatment. The task of the therapist is to utilize this relationship to help the patient through the crisis, at the same time taking care lest the patient remain dependent on the therapist. In crisis intervention, in contrast to brief psychotherapy, it is not necessary for the therapist to promote the conscious participation of the patient in the therapeutic process. Usually the patient's attachment to the therapist is sufficiently strong to permit the therapist to regulate the level of the transference by such techniques as varying the amount of his or her activity, regulating the psychological distance from the patient, and adjusting the length and frequency of the sessions. The aim of the therapist is to diminish the regression of the patient gradually so that by the end of the crisis treatment, manifestations of the regressed transference are no longer evident. Transference interpretations are rarely necessary or useful in accomplishing this goal in the crisis setting. In brief psychotherapy the patient begins treatment much better defended than does the crisis patient. The task of the brief therapist is to permit the transference to develop to the optimal therapeutic level and then to maintain it at that level without permitting it to deepen to a level where separation in a brief period of time might be difficult. The various techniques of brief psychotherapy—the selection of patients, the setting of the time frame, the maintenance of the focus, the regular weekly sessions, the activity of the therapist—all serve to limit regression. The early interpretation of transference phenomena is particularly important in controlling the level of the transfcrence. Throughout the treatment, the patient is made aware of and participates in the monitoring of the various aspects of the therapy.

Crisis intervention is ended when the crisis is over, that is, when the patient feels able to cope with the stressful situation that precipitated the crisis. In crisis intervention issues of termination are often not discussed in the therapy. After the crisis has been resolved, the patient and the therapist often agree that no further treatment is necessary. However, as a result of issues that arose during the course of the crisis intervention, other modalities of treatment may be offered to the patient. Brief psychotherapy is ended when the agreed-upon number of sessions have been held or, in the open-ended brief therapies, when the conflicts have been understood and changes have occurred in the life of the patient. Termination issues are usually dealt with in the treatment, and at times they become central to the therapy. Brief psychotherapy is usually considered a definitive treatment, and further treatment is only rarely offered to the patient at the conclusion of the therapy.

MIXING CRISIS INTERVENTION AND BRIEF PSYCHOTHERAPY

While it is not an uncommon clinical problem to have difficulty determining whether brief or long-term psychotherapy is the treatment of choice for a particular patient, it is rare that one has difficulty in deciding on whether crisis intervention or brief psychotherapy should be used in a given situation. The two modalities are rarely indicated in the same individual. If a person is in crisis, he or she cannot be properly evaluated for brief psychotherapy; if a person can be comfortably evaluated for brief psychotherapy, he or she is probably not in crisis. What does occur is that a patient presents in a crisis, crisis intervention is begun, and as the crisis subsides, it becomes apparent that the patient can benefit from and is suitable for brief psychotherapy.

There are a number of difficulties that can arise from the injudicious mixing of these techniques. During crisis intervention the patient forms a strong positive attachment to the therapist. Because of this, the patient is often eager to please the therapist. This, of course, is useful if the therapist indicates to the patient that, in order to please him or her, the patient should accomplish the goals of the treatment. However, if the question of beginning brief psychotherapy is presented to the patient while he or she is feeling, most likely unconsciously, the need to please the therapist, the patient may agree to undertake a course of treatment for which he or she is not truly motivated. This will often lead to a therapeutic impasse once the brief therapy commences and the patient is faced with a task of self-scrutiny for which he or she is not ready.

Even if the motivation for brief psychotherapy is sufficient, the introduction of the interpretative techniques of brief psychotherapy to a patient still in crisis can be disruptive, both because of the increased anxiety that can result from the interpretations and because the transference may be solidified as a result of the interpretations at a more deeply regressed level than is useful for the brief therapy. It is important that the crisis be fully resolved and that there be little evidence of a regressed relationship between the patient and the therapist before brief psychotherapy is discussed. If there are doubts as to the readiness of the patient to consider objectively the merits of brief psychotherapy, a time interval between the end of crisis intervention and the discussion of further treatment can be set. Sometimes, when there is doubt about the state of the transference, a different therapist can be used for brief psychotherapy than was used for the crisis intervention. (While the above issues are also relevant to beginning long-term psychotherapy after crisis intervention, the problem is more critical with brief psychotherapy. In long-term psychotherapy there is time to sort out the various transference factors, while in brief psychotherapy there will be insufficient time to deal with them.)

There are, of course, many brief psychotherapeutic interventions that cannot be clearly categorized as either crisis intervention or brief psychotherapy. Many of these interventions use some of the elements of both crisis intervention and brief psychotherapy. While it is true that many people are helped with these approaches, there is a danger that in using these mixed forms of therapy a proper evaluation is not carried out before the therapy is undertaken. Thus patients may be treated with a limited approach who would have benefited more from a full course of brief psychotherapy or even long-term psychotherapy had the crisis been resolved first and had a full evaluation followed the resolution of the crisis.

It can be argued that crisis intervention is a suitable term for any psychotherapy that is given to an individual who has an acute problem that he or she experiences with a great deal of affect, and that the more rigid definition of crisis and crisis intervention used in this chapter is too restrictive. It is true that adhering to more stringent criteria leaves many forms of treatment outside the definition, just as the more restrictive diagnostic criteria of DSM-III have left more people without specific diagnoses. The advantage of precision is that it allows clearly defined entities to be studied and compared in a manner that is more meaningful. As has been noted, for many years there were difficulties in clearly separating brief psychotherapy first from psychoanalysis and later from long-term psychotherapy. It was only with well-defined criteria of selection and technique as well as with an understanding of the vicissitudes of the transference throughout the treatment that brief psychotherapy became an established part of the therapeutic armamentarium. Just as it is necessary to distinguish the different approaches to long-term psychotherapy, so too it is essential to delineate the various modalities of brief treatment. At this time enough is known about crisis intervention and brief psychotherapy to define each in terms of selection, technique, and transference manifestations. It is hoped that in the future other modes of brief treatment will also be better understood and defined. It is only by this type of definition that each modality of treatment can be adequately studied and evaluated so that eventually a precise treatment of choice will be available for every clinical situation.

REFERENCES

Alexander, F. (1944). Indications for psychoanalytic therapy. *Bulletin of the New York Academy of Medicine* 20:319–332.

—— (1956). Two forms of regression and their therapeutic implications. *Psychoanalytic Quarterly* 25:178–196.

—— (1965). Psychoanalytic contributions to short-term psychotherapy. In *Short-Term Psychotherapy*, ed. L. Wolberg, pp. 84–126. New York: Grune & Stratton.

Alexander, F., and French, T.M. (1946). *Psychoanalytic Therapy.* New York: Ronald Press.

Balint, M. (1957). *The Doctor, His Patient and the Illness.* New York: International Universities Press.

Breuer, J., and Freud, S. (1895). Studies on hysteria. *Standard Edition* 2:x–305. London: Hogarth Press, 1955.

Burke, J.D., Jr., White, H.S., and Havens, L.L. (1979). Which short-term therapy? *Archives of General Psychiatry* 36:177–186.

Caplan, G. (1964). *Principles of Preventive Psychiatry.* New York: Basic Books.

Chicago Institute for Psychoanalysis (1946). *Proceedings of the Third Psychotherapy Conference.* Chicago: Institute for Psychoanalysis.

Davanloo, H. (1979). Techniques of short-term dynamic psychotherapy. *Psychiatric Clinics of North America* 2:11–22.

——, ed. (1978). *Basic Principles and Techniques in Short-Term Dynamic Psychotherapy.* New York: SP Medical & Scientific Books.

—— (1980). *Short-Term Dynamic Psychotherapy.* New York: Jason Aronson.

Deutsch, F., and Murphy, W.F. (1955). *The Clinical Interview*, 2 vols. New York: International Universities Press.

Eisenstein, S. (1980). The contributions of Franz Alexander. In *Short-Term Dynamic Psychotherapy*, ed. H. Davanloo, pp. 25–41. New York: Jason Aronson.

Ferenczi, S. (1952). *Further Contributions to the Theory and Technique of Psycho-Analysis.* New York: Basic Books.

Ferenczi, S., and Rank, O. (1925). *The Development of Psycho-analysis*. New York: Nervous & Mental Disease Publishing Company.

Flegenheimer, W.V. (1978). The patient–therapist relationship in crisis intervention. *Journal of Clinical Psychiatry* 39:348–350.

—— (1979). Short-term therapy (letter to the editor). *American Journal of Psychiatry* 136:992.

Freud, S. (1905). A case of hysteria. *Standard Edition* 7:7–122. London: Hogarth Press, 1953.

—— (1919). Advances in psycho-analytic therapy. *Standard Edition* 17:159–168. London: Hogarth Press, 1955.

—— (1937). Analysis terminable and interminable. *Standard Edition* 23:216–253. London: Hogarth Press, 1964.

Golden, C. (1978). Implications of the interviewer's technique on selection criteria. In *Basic Principles and Techniques in Short-Term Dynamic Psychotherapy*, ed. H. Davanloo, pp. 269–290. New York: SP Medical & Scientific Books.

Jones, E. (1957). *The Life and Work of Sigmund Freud*, vol. 3. New York: Basic Books.

Lindemann, E. (1944). Symptomatology and management of acute grief. *American Journal of Psychiatry* 101:141–148.

Macalpine, I. (1950). The development of the transference. *Psychoanalytic Quarterly* 19:501–539.

Malan, D.H. (1963). *A Study of Brief Psychotherapy*. New York: Plenum.

—— (1976a). *The Frontier of Brief Psychotherapy*. New York: Plenum.

—— (1976b). *Towards the Validation of Dynamic Psychotherapy*. New York: Plenum.

Mann, J. (1973). *Time-Limited Psychotherapy*. Cambridge, MA: Harvard University Press.

Mann, J., and Goldman, R. (1982). *A Casebook in Time-Limited Psychotherapy*. New York: McGraw-Hill.

Marmor, J. (1979). Short-term dynamic psychotherapy. *American Journal of Psychiatry* 136:149–155.

—— (1980). Crisis intervention and short-term dynamic psycho-therapy. In *Short-Term Dynamic Psychotherapy*, ed. H. Davanloo, pp. 237–243. New York: Jason Aronson.

Shafer, R. (1973). Termination of brief psychoanalytic psycho-therapy. *International Journal of Psychoanalytic Psychotherapy* 2:135–148.

Sifneos, P.E. (1967). Two different kinds of psychotherapy of short duration. *American Journal of Psychiatry* 123:1069–1074.

——— (1972). *Short-Term Psychotherapy and Emotional Crisis.* Cambridge, MA: Harvard University Press.

——— (1979). *Short-Term Dynamic Psychotherapy.* New York: Plenum.

Sterba, R. (1951). A case of brief psychotherapy by Sigmund Freud. *Psychoanalytic Review* 38:75–80.

Strupp, H.H., and Hadley, S.W. (1979). Specific versus nonspecific factors in psychotherapy: A controlled study of outcome. *Archives of General Psychiatry* 36:1125–1136.

Wolberg, L.R. (1965). *Short-Term Psychotherapy.* New York: Grune & Stratton.

——— (1977). *The Technique of Psychotherapy*, 3rd ed. New York: Grune & Stratton.

——— (1980). *Handbook of Short-Term Psychotherapy.* New York: Thieme-Stratton.

APPENDIX:
ANNOTATED
BIBLIOGRAPHY

Alexander, F., and French, T.M. (1946). *Psychoanalytic Therapy.* New York: Ronald Press.

This classic book, written by Alexander and his coworkers, can still be read with profit by anyone interested in psychoanalytically oriented psychotherapy. It is rich in clinical insights and case material, covering most aspects of psychotherapy. While the individual chapters are clearly written, the book is somewhat marred by a lack of overall organization. Because Alexander emphasizes the similarities among all forms of psychotherapy, it can be difficult for the reader to distinguish the differences in selection criteria and technique between long-term and brief psychotherapy. (For a review of the contents of the book, see the section on Alexander in Chapter 2.)

Davanloo, H., ed. (1978). *Basic Principles and Techniques in Short-Term Dynamic Psychotherapy.* New York: SP Medical & Scientific Books.

Davanloo, H., ed. (1980). *Short-Term Dynamic Psychotherapy.* New York: Jason Aronson.

The first of these books is based on material from the First and Second International Symposia and Workshops on Short-Term Dynamic Psychotherapy held in Montreal in 1975 and 1976. The second book is based on the Third International Symposium held in Los Angeles in 1977. The books consist of essays by various contributors and transcripts of interviews with patients. Like most books derived from meetings, the

197

content is quite uneven. Davanloo has published little of his work in a systematic fashion. His contributions to the didactic portions of these books give some indication of his thinking about brief psychotherapy. The extensive verbatim clinical excerpts of interviews conducted by Davanloo, Malan, and Sifneos are excellent. A careful study of Davanloo's transcripts will give the reader a good picture of what Davanloo actually does with patients and what makes his therapy so unique. While Malan has published extensive case material elsewhere (see below), these books provide the only verbatim transcripts of Malan interviewing patients heretofore published. These transcripts give a good picture of Malan's style. Sifneos has published verbatim transcripts elsewhere (see below); his contributions to these books are additional examples of his way of working with patients.

Malan, D.H. (1976). *The Frontier of Brief Psychotherapy*. New York: Plenum.

Malan writes extremely well. Unfortunately his major book on brief psychotherapy is quite difficult to read because of organizational problems. It is sometimes hard for the reader to separate the extensive material on Malan's research project from his clinical conclusions. However, careful study of this book and the companion volume (see below) will provide the reader with a wealth of data on Malan's excellent psychotherapy research and follow-up studies as well as picture of what Malan's therapy is actually like. In this book, 18 case histories are presented in some detail, including material on presenting complaints, past history, dynamic factors, treatment issues, and long-term follow-up interviews. No verbatim transcripts are included.

Malan, D.H. (1976). *Towards the Validation of Dynamic Psychotherapy*. New York: Plenum.

This book provides further information about Malan's research, of interest mainly to those concerned with the methodology of psychotherapy research. However the 12 case histories, in the same format as those described above, will be of interest to the clinician.

Mandel, H.P. (1981). *Short-Term Psychotherapy and Brief Treatment Techniques. An Annotated Bibliography 1920–1980.* New York: Plenum.

This annotated bibliography of 1552 entries covering all aspects of brief psychotherapy is a useful reference work. Each entry is followed by a brief summary of the content of the article or book. The entries are arranged alphabetically by author and the subject index is quite limited, so this book will be mainly helpful when the author is known and information is desired about the content of his work. (For a bibliography arranged according to subject, see Small below.)

Mann, J. (1973). *Time-Limited Psychotherapy.* Cambridge, MA: Harvard University Press.

This book is a model of its kind. In a brief number of pages a complete system of psychotherapy, as well as its rationale, is set forth with adequate clinical examples. In addition, a nearly complete verbatim transcript of an entire 12-session therapy is included. Upon completing this book, the reader will have a good understanding of Mann's method of brief psychotherapy.

Mann, J., and Goldman, R. (1982). *A Casebook in Time-Limited Psychotherapy.* New York: McGraw-Hill.

In this later work, Mann extends his concept of the central issue and expands his criteria for selecting patients. The case material, which comprises the major portion of the book, shows the wide application of this technique. Five cases are presented in some detail.

Sifneos, P. (1972). *Short-Term Psychotherapy and Emotional Crisis.* Cambridge, MA: Harvard University Press.

This book clearly presents Sifneos's system of brief therapy. There is extensive and varied clinical material, including verbatim transcripts. The book's organization is somewhat marred by the inclusion of sections on crisis intervention, but the reader can easily separate the material on crisis intervention from that on brief psychotherapy.

Sifneos, P. (1979). *Short-Term Dynamic Psychotherapy*. New York:
     Plenum.

In this book, Sifneos again describes his technique in detail,
providing extensive clinical examples and verbatim transcripts.

Small, L. (1979). *The Briefer Psychotherapies*, rev. ed. New York:
     Brunner/Mazel.

This book is essentially an annotated bibliography of 520 references. The material is presented in a narrative style, with
chapters devoted to various topics in the field. This book is
most useful for those seeking references to a particular subject. (For an annotated bibliography arranged according to
author, see Mandel above.)

Wolberg, L.R. (1980). *Handbook of Short-Term Psychotherapy*.
     New York: Thieme-Stratton.

This book presents both an overview of the field and a descrip-
tion of Wolberg's own technique of brief psychotherapy. While
the book contains a wealth of information, it may be difficult
for the reader seeking to learn Wolberg's technique to separate
the specific from the general. There are numerous clinical
vignettes and some verbatim transcripts, but no extensive
example of a case treated by Wolberg's method is included in
the book.

INDEX

About the Author

Walter V. Flegenheimer, M.D., is Assistant Clinical Professor of Psychiatry at the Mount Sinai School of Medicine. For ten years he was associated with the Brief Psychotherapy Research Project at the Beth Israel Medical Center in New York City; he contributed to many presentations and publications of that group.